THE TAMING
OF THE FRONTIER

EL PASO IN 1868

THE TAMING
OF THE FRONTIER

**EL PASO : OGDEN : DENVER : ST. PAUL
SAN FRANCISCO : PORTLAND : KANSAS CITY
CHEYENNE : SAN ANTONIO : LOS ANGELES**

BY TEN AUTHORS

EDITED BY
DUNCAN AIKMAN

Essay Index Reprint Series

BOOKS FOR LIBRARIES PRESS, INC.
FREEPORT, NEW YORK

First Published 1925
Reprinted 1967

LIBRARY OF CONGRESS CATALOG CARD NUMBER: 67-26711

978
Ai 4 t
65557
april 1969

PRINTED IN THE UNITED STATES OF AMERICA

CONTENTS

ILLUSTRATIONS

CONTRIBUTORS

OWEN P. WHITE, though he is now in his forties, is the oldest inhabitant of American parentage born in El Paso. He is the author of "Them Was the Days," a retrospect of frontier life, and "Out of the Desert," a history of El Paso, and is a frequent contributor to the American Mercury. At present he is on the staff of the New York Times.

BERNARD DE VOTO, a native of Utah, is an instructor in English at Northwestern University. His first novel, "The Crooked Mile," was published in 1924.

GEORGE LOOMS is a former dramatic editor of Denver newspapers and is the author of three novels: "Stubble," "John No-Brawn," and "The Caraways."

IDWAL JONES is an ex-machinist and a writer of special articles on the San Francisco Examiner. His first novel, dealing with gypsy life in America in the 1850's, will be published in the fall of 1925.

MRS. GRACE FLANDRAU, a native of St. Paul, is the author of two novels, "Being Respectable" and "Entranced."

DEAN COLLINS is a feature writer for the Portland (Ore.) Telegram and a frequent contributor to magazines.

HENRY J. HASKELL is chief editorial writer of the Kansas City Star. He is a contributor to The World's Work, The Outlook, and The Independent.

MRS. DORA NEILL RAYMOND, a native Texan, is assistant professor of history in Sweetbriar College, Virginia. She is the author of "British Policy and Opinion during the Franco-Prussian War" and "The Political Career of Lord Byron."

PAUL JORDAN-SMITH, a Californian of long residence, is the author of a book of essays, "On Strange Altars," and two novels, "Cables of Cobweb" and "Nomad."

CARY ABBOTT is a native of Cheyenne and a former editor of the Yale Literary Magazine.

The publishers are indebted to the editors of The American Mercury for permission to reprint "El Paso" by Owen P. White and "San Francisco" by Idwal Jones.

INTRODUCTION

The legend of the standardization of American cities is easy to believe. There is an appalling amount of supporting evidence. While New Orleans hacks down its "galleries" to make room for office buildings, Keokuk imports "California-Spanish" bungalows and Santa Barbara imports Iowans. Spokane and Peoria and El Paso function with impressive efficiency as each other's unconscious mimics. There is justice even in the cruel saying that, despite the fame of its criminal intelligentsia, Chicago is but the Los Angeles of the Great Lakes region.

Serious defenders of vivacity and variety in our national life have good grounds for complaining to the police about wanton cruelties inflicted by all this high pressure uniformity upon that unfortunate animal once called the American individual. What chance has he in a civilization which only asks that he get into a groove and never under any provocation flop out of it? How can he survive except in a secret and ironic anguish in a society which demands that as go-getter, up-lifter, high-powered executive, fundamentalist, Labor Union business agent, home town booster, Yale alumnus, or Country Club play boy, he run one hundred per cent true to type seven days a week?

One cannot read of these ten cities, or, indeed, be alive in any American city today without realizing how the gods of individualism in both personal and community life have been thrown down to make way for the gods of standardization. Out in the West especially, where a generation or two ago the pioneer imposed his individuality upon raw and uncouth towns at the point of his six-shooter, today the group prejudices of boosters and breeders to type impose their pet conformities with gestures scarcely less ferocious. Laugh publicly and rationally at the slogans and statistics of the Boosterburg Chamber of Commerce and you will see.

But is all this merely a truth of temporary appearances, or one of those devastatingly eternal truths from which there is no escape short of translation to a reasonably variegated Hades?

These articles supply an answer, and a glimmer of encouragement.

Standardized as these ten western cities are, where there was so little of ancient and deep-rooted tradition to keep off the coming of uniformity, they are by no means ten finished Boosterburgs.

Drawing upon some inexhaustible blandness in her ancestral heritage, San Antonio has fought the boosters and their conformities to a standstill. No blows exchanged, no rough stuff. It is merely as if a travelling drummer or the Rev. Dr. Sunday had hoarsely criticized the gown of a princess, and she, not deigning to attend his discourse directly,

had thereafter worn the garment with a slightly
more studied carelessness.

In San Francisco, it is true, the modern Appolyon fills the streets more and more with the
stench of his realtorian ethics, the windy sound of
his Kiwanian back-slappings and of Lions roaring
booster slogans in chorus. But San Francisco still
fights Appolyon in the name of ancient and fantastic gayeties; in the name of personal idiosyncrasies
too acid to merge easily with the digestive fluids of
Main Street which would, if they could, convert us
all to the same chemical substance.

Appolyon may have begotten a Boosterburg
upon San Francisco. But the damsel's term is
not due yet, and, considering her sophistication and
the hectic life she leads, there may be a mishap.

The other eight cities are perhaps further gone
along the Boosterburg way. Yet even so, much
is to be said for them. The state they have attained,
is the same, let it be granted: Kansas City and Los
Angeles are two peas of slightly different size and
structural appearance from the same pod. But
into this very sameness, they have grown by what
different processes, with what varying motives!

Portland to preserve the good name of her soiled
Puritanism by a noisy display of it! Denver seeking in intolerant conformity an effective check upon
an individualism once intolerably and criminally
violent! Los Angeles realizing that that municipal
standardization which makes the loudest noise upon
this planet will best qualify its realtors financially
to entertain angels of Hollywood! Ogden resolute

with the smug cunning of its stupidity to make a fat living out of conformity while the chance lasts! El Paso whipped on by the inferiority complex of a small and remote community to risk all on doing, however clumsily, "the right thing"! Kansas City struggling pathetically and inharmoniously, but more encouragingly than some others, to determine what the "right thing" is!

For these are, despite their more or less common ending, varied tales—fully as varied as the million and one romances which have concluded "and so they were married." Fiction apart, that is a coincidence which has, by proof in the vital statistics, occurred in the lives of several billion historical persons. May there not be a similar biological impulse, a similar necessity of growth and development, which requires one to chronicle of a certain period in the lives of cities—— "and so they were standardized?"

So it would seem from these ten chronicles of progression toward a goal at least as appalling and dangerous to individuality as is matrimony itself.

Yet we have the modern novel to thank for the revelation that the phrase, "and so they were married," is by no means the end of the story, or even the end of diversity.

May it not be thus also with the melancholy conclusion of so many of these histories? May not these very diverse motives which within living memory have pushed ten of our outstanding western cities into a standardization both odious and amusing to contemplate, push them onward, when the momentary coincidence has passed, into an individualism as sharply diverse as that of the Italian cities of the 15th century?

We shall know better when our grandchildren contribute their sequel to this symposium. Meanwhile, may not the very vigor and dash of these protests against our sterile urban conformities be signs from the God of cats who walk by themselves?

THE EDITOR.

EL PASO:
"THE RIGHT THING" ON THE FRONTIER
By
Owen P. White

THE TAMING
OF THE FRONTIER

EL PASO

A S I look back over the few short years that intervene between the reign of Ben Dowell, El Paso's first potentate, and that of Dick Dudley, its present dictator, and compare the paved, pious and stolid city of to-day with the rough, uncouth and very gay town in which I was born, I cannot refrain from heaving a deep and comprehensive wheeze of regret. Where life was once cheerful, filled with alarms and worth living, it is now flat, decorous and commonplace; where men were once publicly and delightfully naughty and openly belli-cose they are now only surreptitiously so; where the leading citizens once wore six-shooters and Win-chesters they now wear wrist watches and golf sticks, and where—God save the race!—the com-munal sports, in days past, were wont to drink hard liquor out of the original carboys and to play poker with the North Star as the limit they now absorb coca-cola with a dash of *tequila* in it, and bet on mah jong at a twentieth of a cent a point.

It's pathetic. It really is. And it began in

3

1873. Before that calamitous year, from time im-
memorial, all the residents of El Paso, of both
sexes, had been in the habit of bathing freely,
openly and nakedly, in the sight of God and anybody else who cared to look, in the irrigation ditches
that ran hither and yon through the adjacent fields
and vineyards. It was a delightfully primitive and
intimate custom; one which everybody enjoyed and
indulged in without thought of evil or blush of
shame. And then, in the year mentioned, suddenly
and with no adequate reason, El Paso, with its
three combined saloons and gambling houses, its
one hotel, its two stage stations and horse corrals
and its three stores, took unto itself the idea that it
would some day become a great city, and in anticipation thereof held an election. As was right and
proper, Uncle Ben Dowell, whose saloon was the
biggest in town, was chosen mayor, and to assist
him he was given a board of six aldermen whose
secular occupations ran all the way from the un-
profitable one of an Episcopal minister out of a
job to the lucrative one of a Jewish merchant. Immediately these seven men, newly intrusted with
legislative control over the liberties of their fellow
citizens, proceeded to commit a deed of imperishable shame by writing in large, flaring letters on
page one, in book one, of the Ordinances of the
City of El Paso the words "Thou shalt not!" It
became a high crime and misdemeanor for any person, male or female, brown or white, married or
single, to wade, paddle, dive, duck or swim in the
waters of any irrigation ditch within the corporate

limits of the city! Civilization had arrived with a bang. The old days were no more.

El Paso, in those years, was not much to look at. Mud, mere primitive mud, mixed with straw and baked in the sun, was all that the town was made of, and although all the other settlements along the Rio Grande had their mission churches, it had none, and so there was no belfry on the sky-line to break the monotony of the low, flat-roofed houses.

But the location of the town, even though it was forgotten by the men of God, made it important in the eyes of certain other men. Standing in the doorway of his saloon and looking to the north and south, Uncle Ben Dowell, in his leisure moments, could allow his gaze to wander along a trail—the oldest in the United States—which wended its adventurous way through the two thousand miles of perils that separated Santa Fé in New Mexico from the City of Mexico down in the old country. And looking in the other direction, to the east and west, he could see the celebrated Butterworth stage route, which meandered along over its sandy and sinuous course clear through from San Antonio to the Pacific Coast. Thus El Paso stood exactly, to the very inch almost, at the cross-roads formed by two great continental trails. It is due to this one unassisted fact that the town owes its origin and also—with humble apologies to those who fancy that it will cease to function as soon as they pass on—its present existence. Over these two great trails came the stages by which El Paso kept in uncertain touch with the rest of the world, and from one of these stages, every now and then, some stranger would descend.

Those were the days when no man in the Southwest asked any other man where he came from or what his business was. El Paso, indeed, had no credentials of her own to exhibit to strangers and so she asked none from them. Any visitor who dropped in was free to go as far as he liked so long as he paid his way, restrained his curiosity, and refrained from entering into an alliance with the private soul-mate of a permanent resident. For those who, either because they were tired of life or because they were ignorant or reckless, disregarded these proprieties there was a cemetery provided. As for the regular residents of the place—and there were only twenty-five or thirty Americans among them, the rest being Mexicans who cultivated the grape to turn it into wine and *aguardiente*—they did practically nothing except watch for dust clouds along the mesa rim, play monte, poker or faro, bet on straight-away horse races and cock fights, and drink the beverages composed by the Mexicans.

During this period of its life El Paso, under the rule of Ben Dowell, J. F. Crosby, Joseph Magoffin, Sam Schutz, Parson Tays, and James Hague, was hard but it was not vicious. Men lived loose, irregular and immoral lives because they lived natural ones. There were some laws, true enough— those of the State, the nation and God—but inasmuch as none of these authorities kept a representative on hand to enforce them the duty of preserving his life and protecting his property devolved upon each individual. The result was that men were indubitably he; they read each other's eyes and not the Book, and a word was as good as a bond. But Utopias, of course, never last, and an end had to come to this one. Ever since 1859 El Paso had been marked on the map of progress as a railroad center. Frémont and even the great Baron von Humboldt had forecast a great future for the little cluster of mud huts. But it was not until 1879 that anything of a definite nature occurred. In that year, suddenly and thrillingly, four great railroad trunk lines—not merely one, but four—began to build feverishly in the direction of Ben Dowell's saloon, and the moment it became generally known that his bar was to become an important junction, men of all classes, from all parts of the United States, began to hasten to it. These newcomers, alas, were not like their heroic predecessors. They were of a lesser and ignobler breed. They were border parasites coming in to prey upon the railroad payrolls. At first these men, and the women who were with them, came in slowly, but as the railheads gradually drew nearer and nearer the influx increased, until by the middle of 1880 people were arriving at the rate of hundreds a day. They came in ambulances, in buggies, in wagons, on foot and on horseback; they ate what they could get; they slept any- and every-where they worked during the day erecting adobe houses to live in and caroused joyously through most of the night. In short, El Paso had a boom and everybody was happy and hilarious, especially the old-timers who had waited so long.

But their joy was soon mixed with sorrow. Within a few months after the beginning of the rush, and almost a year before the first railroad finally reached the town, the city fathers found that they were up against a new and a hard proposition. The former bad men, the gun-toters of the plains, the Mexican bandits, the Apache Indians and the brown-skinned señoritas who loved for cash were species which they knew how to handle. But when it came to managing the new element in the population, made up principally of crooks who had taken their Ph.D. and LL.D. degrees in the great metropolises of the East, they found themselves stumped. Murders which were unwarranted and unethical, even from the free and easy point of view of the frontier, became too frequent to be tolerated, and petty criminals, a class heretofore unknown to the Southwest, began to operate enormously. Life and property thus became unsafe, and so El Paso once again organized itself for the protection of its honest citizens, and a newly elected council set about looking for a man upon whom to wish the job of city marshal.

The gentleman finally honored with this office was a warlike character by the name of Campbell and, in order that his administration might be made a complete success, he was given an assistant in the person of one Bill Johnson. To the two was intrusted the business of putting the fear of God and a respect for the Constitution into the hearts of El Paso's new and unregenerate citizenry. Meanwhile, the town had begun to grow in size as well as in population. In place of one short street and three saloons it now had two pretentious avenues and between twenty and thirty drinking resorts. In place of being fed at two *chile* joints, the populace ate in style at half a dozen Chinese restaurants. And now it boasted, too, of several new dance halls, with dirt floors, and two variety theaters, one of which, the Coliseum, owned by the Manning brothers, was the largest in the West.

Over the social activity for which these suddenly acquired municipal improvements furnished a background, Marshal Campbell and his able assistant were supposed to exert a restraining influence. But they never did. On the contrary, under their control the town went from bad to worse, until at the end of a month or two a condition prevailed which made Ben Dowell and Joseph Magoffin and Samuel Schutz, who had been on the border since '59, and who thought they knew something about real wickedness, blush for shame at the contemplation of their own innocence. Campbell struck up an intimate friendship with the Manning brothers and with the proprietors of the other resorts and would arrest none of their patrons, and Johnson stayed drunk all the time; in consequence, the new town lock-up stood untenanted. The new element in the population, in brief, did as it pleased, and since its tastes ran largely to robbery, riot and bloodshed, it soon became apparent to all right-thinking men that something had to be done.

Finally the mayor sent for the marshal and demanded a show-down. Campbell replied by declaring that his salary was not large enough to justify him in wasting any more energy on his job than he was already putting into it, but he assured his Honor that an increase in pay would bring about an increase in the number of incarcerations. Whereupon, much to his surprise and disgust and to the chagrin of his friends, he was promptly fired and his badge and baton transferred to his inebriated assistant. Then the whole town, with the new marshal and his former chief in the van of the drinkers, went on a spree. This lasted for about a month and then, as a wind-up, ex-Marshal Campbell and his friends proceeded to carry out a plan they had formed for restoring him to his old dignity. Shorn of detail, this plan was to shoot up the entire town at one great blast and so scare the mayor into hiring Campbell again, and at his own figure.

Accordingly, at two o'clock one morning, when all communal festivities were at their height, when love looked love to eyes that spoke invitation, when the men on the graveyard shift in the gambling halls were ready to take their places, when the bartenders, working hard, were telling the line to form to the right, and when the girls in the variety theaters were most industriously a-hoof, the word was given and hell was let loose. In every saloon, dance hall and chink restaurant in the town and in both of the variety theaters it was the same. No place was spared. Every light in El Paso went out under a fusillade of shots and in the ensuing darkness, as men cursed and women screamed, all sorts of herculean deviltries were engaged in. Men were assaulted and robbed, girls were pinched and kissed, and many an eminent citizen was sent home on the run with six-shooter bullets kicking up the dust under his heels. Nowhere in the West had the shooting-up process ever been carried out with such scientific thoroughness. When it was over the conspirators relighted a few kerosene lamps in the least damaged of the saloons, pulled the bartenders out from their holes, and, soothed by their ministrations, sat around and waited for daylight to arrive, confident that the mayor and all others concerned were by now convinced that Campbell, and Campbell alone, could handle the situation.

But the mayor was made of harder stuff. Next morning, when the six-shooter smoke had cleared away and men were beginning to poke their noses out of the doors of their shacks, he sprung a surprise of his own. Instead of sending for the discharged marshal and reinstating him in office he did something that was entirely unheard of. He sent down to Ysleta, a small settlement thirteen miles away on the Rio Grande, where a camp of Texas rangers was located, and asked that a detachment be sent up to police the town until he could make some arrangement to handle it himself. His call was promptly answered. Capt. J. B. Gillett, than whom no better man ever stuck foot in a stirrup, came galloping in at the head of his men, and from that time on peace and quiet prevailed.

But as the rangers were State officers whose business it was to patrol the frontier and not to do police duty in towns, they were lent to the mayor for the period of the emergency only, and so the council found itself under the necessity of finding a man to fill Campbell's place permanently. He appeared almost at once, and, as it seemed to the harassed burghers, almost providentially. His name was Dallas Stoudenmire. Accompanied by his brother-in-law, Doc Cummings, he came down from New Mexico, called upon the mayor, presented his credentials, asked that he be made custodian of the peace, and was forthwith given the job and told to go to it.

Stoudenmire was a German blond, six feet four inches in height, weighing two hundred pounds and carrying two six-shooters. When he was told to go to it, he went. Bill Johnson had never been removed from office officially, even while the rangers were in town, but this trifling omission made no difference to the new head of the *Polizei*. The moment he pinned on his badge of office he called upon Johnson and demanded the keys to the jail. The drunkard, not being acquainted with Stoudenmire, and also, perhaps, still thinking that he had some legal rights, refused to deliver them. Thereupon the giant seized him by the collar, turned him wrong side up, and shook him until the keys dropped from his pocket. For a day or two after this everything was serene. Then, presumably when Stoudenmire was not around to take a hand in the fray, his brother-in-law, Doc Cummings, was killed in a gun fight following an altercation with the Manning brothers. This killing, for which Jim Manning, whose bartender and not he was probably guilty, was tried and acquitted on a plea of self-defense, resulted in an enmity between Stoudenmire and the Mannings which brought bloody results.

The first trouble, coming within a week, presented itself to the new marshal as a fortuitous opportunity to display his prowess and place himself squarely before the connoisseurs of the town. An unimportant inquest had been held over the carcasses of two Mexicans, found murdered on the outskirts of the town. At its conclusion a quarrel arose between Johnnie Hale, an old resident and a close friend of the Manning brothers, and a man named Gus Krempkau. For the purpose of terminating the argument, and probably desiring to get home for lunch, Hale pulled out his artillery and shot Krempkau dead. Immediately Stoudenmire, who had come up and joined the crowd, went into action. With his first shot he killed a Mexican who looked as if he was about to pull a gun, with his second he sent Johnnie Hale's soul winging to the angels, and then, turning just in time to see ex-Marshal Campbell, who was directly behind him, reach for his weapon, he killed him too.

This spectacular masterpiece at once established his reputation. Three men with three shots, anywhere in the Southwest in those days, constituted an almost perfect score and thereafter, for a few weeks, the marshal was allowed to lead an uneventful and undisturbed life. During these weeks the town was quieter than it had ever been before, and the town lock-up, unused during the Campbell-Johnson administration, nightly sheltered swarms of felons upon whom the hand of the law, as represented by the mighty grip of Dallas Stoudenmire, had been ruthlessly laid. This activity, however, only served to increase the hatred that the sporting element harbored against Stoudenmire. It was bad for business to have men put in jail who still had money in their pockets and were drunk enough to spend it. Therefore, combining the high motive of business expediency with the more archaic one of revenge, the Campbell crowd got together and decided to put Stoudenmire out of the way. For that purpose they made use of the animosity of Bill Johnson. Bill was filled with fighting whiskey and it was suggested to him that he ought, in common decency, to kill Stoudenmire. Hadn't the marshal treated him like a Mexican when he shook the keys out of his pocket?

Bill, thus plied with persuasions, finally agreed. It was a dark night, a fine one for a murder, and he was given a double-barreled gun loaded with buck shot, and led to a point across the road from Ben Dowell's saloon. At this place, which is now the intersection of the two principal business streets of El Paso, there stood a pile of bricks to be used in the erection of the town's first brick building, and behind it Johnson secreted himself to await his victim. When he went into ambush Stoudenmire, whose movements were being closely watched, was down at the Acme Saloon, but it was well known that he would soon make his evening round of the town. It was not long before his enemies, a number of whom had hidden themselves across the road from Johnson's hiding place, saw him approaching, and when he was within twenty feet of the brick pile they saw Johnson rise up behind it and fire both barrels of his gun. But either because he was suffering from a severe attack of buck ague or stage fright, or because he was unsteady from too much whiskey, he missed. Then Stoudenmire, drawing his pistol, quickly filled the would-be assassin's body with bullets. The men on the other side of the road now opened fire on him, wounding him in the foot, but, drawing another gun, he charged them head on and quickly put them to flight.

From that day until he resigned from office Stoudenmire held imperial sway over El Paso. He kept order, sometimes by shooting his' man, sometimes by merely bringing down his gun upon the offender's head. Unluckily, like most men of his class and time, he had one great fault. He was a copious drinker and, although he could carry an almost incredible cargo without loss of his faculties, there were still times when it would get the better of him and he would become dangerous even to his friends. Finally, after a year of service during which he wrote his name, principally with blood, upon the imperishable records of El Paso, he was politely asked to resign, and the Captain Gillett already mentioned was appointed to succeed him. Within a few months after his resignation Stoudenmire was killed in a gun fight with two of the Mannings, Jim Manning, as usual, being tried for the murder and acquitted on his regular plea of self-defense.

In 1881, shortly before Stoudenmire resigned, the first railroad reached the town and immediately, over night almost, its entire aspect underwent a second change. Physically the metamorphosis was striking. Before the locomotives puffed their way in there had been only one brick building, no board floors, and according to legend, only two glass windows in the place. Such Babylonish luxuries as mahogany fixtures in the saloons and square pianos in the dance halls were unknown. But within less than a year all of these deficiencies, as well as some others of which the town had been theretofore ignorant, had been supplied. Brick buildings began to take the place of the old adobe ones; ornate bar equipment and costly gambling tables replaced the makeshift devices formerly in use; men who had never before tripped the light fantastic on anything but Mother Earth could now hear the tapping of their own boot heels, and a new element, a peroxided, hand-decorated, female one, recruited in the East and Middle West and shipped in by the carload, came to supplant the brown-skinned, black-eyed, dusky-haired señoritas of the day before. Night life in the town now became more alluring than it had ever been.

A wonderful prosperity was about to come to the
Southwest, and Vice, knowing that the pickings
were going to be easy, garbed itself becomingly for
the harvest and assumed an air of affluence. The
blonde women wore beautiful gowns—cut too high
and too low, but beautiful none the less; the bartenders discarded their flannel shirts and corduroy
pants and began to wear white jackets and thou-
sand-dollar diamonds; and the gambling fraternity
blossomed out in all the glory of imported tailor-
made garments and kept women.

Behind all this was the constant thought of
money. Up to the time when the news that the
railroads were on the way had changed a village
that was actually admirable for the heroic quality
of its badness into a border town whose population
was made up largely of abject apostles of vice,
nobody had cared very much for cash. Money had
been a convenience but not a necessity. A man's
social standing had then depended much more upon
his capacity for handling his liquor and his ability
to shoot straight than upon the number of fifty or
hundred dollar bills that he could display to a
sordid public. In the pre-railroad days money was
not the *summum bonum* of the El Pasoans. But
it became so the moment the boom was under way.

In addition to unloading blondes, bar fixtures
and building materials, the trains also began to
deliver a class of men who came for the purpose of
embarking in more or less legitimate business.
These newcomers became just as busy as the sports.
They set about making the town a good one for

trade, as the sporting fraternity had already made it a good one—the best in the Southwest—for entertainment. Thus El Paso soon became the Mecca towards which every honest soul in the Southwest who had his pockets full turned at least once and usually several times a year. The diamond-studded bartenders, the beautifully tailored gamblers and the wonderfully painted ladies extended to the visitors, one and all, an invitation to enjoy themselves. They all came and they all had a good time. The resorts were open twenty-four hours a day, seven days a week. Thus, for more than twenty years, ranch owners, cow-punchers, miners, prospectors, traveling men and merchants from all over Texas, Arizona and New Mexico made an annual pilgrimage to El Paso, ostensibly to transact business, but really to be painlessly relieved of their accumulated wealth.

Men who had entered into legitimate business saw it increase wonderfully; they began to grow rich. Corner lots which had been valueless a short time before made fortunes for old-timers who had held on to them, and showered down a golden harvest upon delegations of realtors from Missouri, and upon a trio from Tennessee who had come in early enough in the game to grab some choice locations. The advance in cattle prices turned former cowpunchers into plutocrats; prospect holes out in Arizona and up in New Mexico transformed their previously poverty-stricken owners into millionaires. Everybody made money, and everybody was happy. El Paso grew; the sporting element continued to prosper; the derby hat and the white collar became tolerated; marriage licenses began to be issued with some degree of regularity; ministers of the gospel made their appearance; church spires pierced the heavens. And then the war was on!

For the first few years there was only desultory skirmishing. But in 1894 there began a struggle which soon had most of El Paso's "better" element side-stepping with as much agility as a flea shows in hopping. By better element, of course, I mean that portion of the population which was not engaged directly in operating saloons, gambling houses, dance halls, variety theaters or stews. Naturally, this element was large, but if I were to say, in place of "directly operating," "interested in" or "profiting by," the number, I fear, would be somewhat reduced. In fact, everybody in El Paso, and even the city itself, was deeply involved with the sporting element. For years the revenues derived from licensing gambling houses, dance halls and bawdy houses ran the city, thus relieving the taxpayers of a heavy burden and allowing the pious to contribute heavily to foreign missions and Bible societies. But that was not all. In addition to helping the city fathers with their financial problem El Paso's sports did the business men of the community a more direct service. They made the town highly attractive to all the citizens of the adjacent States, and brought in thousands to buy bolts of calico, picks, shovels and barrels of dill pickles who might have just as well placed their

orders in Denver or Los Angeles. These customers came in person, transacted their business
during the day, and then at night, as a matter of
hospitality, they were shown the town, chaperoned,
as a rule, by the merchant or banker or broker with
whom they had had their dealings. Of course, the
El Paso business men didn't like this duty—in
fact, they hated it—but as it was established by
custom they performed it uncomplainingly, and,
as a matter of additional politeness went as far as
their visiting friends in the way of having a good
time.

Thus, during the intensely busy years between
1881 and 1904, when the doors of the "public"
gambling houses and dance halls were closed forever, many of the prominent citizens of the town
acquired an indirect interest in the operation of
the communal dens of iniquity, and were thus unable to lend their whole-hearted support to the
closing movement. Their indignation had to be
concealed. It was well enough for a man to
agree with his wife when she said to him at the
breakfast table: "George, dear, this is a hell of
a place to raise children," but it was an entirely different matter when George got down to his office
and checked up his books. There he found that
if the rent didn't come in from the saloon building that he owned on the corner, he wouldn't be
able to come across with that thousand dollar subscription to the new Methodist Church; that if
Madame X and her girls didn't pay for the gaudy
gowns bought last month he couldn't settle for

the simple little things that his own girls, under-
going a polishing treatment on the Hudson, said
that they had to have; that if Old Man Taylor,
the gambler, didn't kick in with the agreed price
for four corner lots, the wife couldn't, during the
coming social season, tilt her head at the right
angle.

Altogether, it was a difficult situation for Christian men. It was met by turning it into a political
issue. Vice entrenched itself for a siege and the
reformers, few at first but strong in spirit, formed
for the assault. It was a long and beautiful battle
and at the end of ten years the reformers got the
decision. After that the blonde heads of the ladies
from Utah Street were no longer to be seen in the
dress circle at the old Myar Opera House, dis-
tracting the attention of the men from the play
upon the stage; the whir of the roulette wheel and
the rattle of the poker chip no longer called busy
merchants from the barroom to the upper floor of
the Gem Saloon, and the banging of the piano no
more invited the transient cowpuncher and the itinerant prospector into the caressing arms of the
frescoed beauties of Louis Vidal's dance hall.
These things were gone, gone never to return!
What took their place?

They took their own place. That is to say, they
took a legal but not a physical departure from the
town. El Paso became, externally, very decorous,
and the reformers, lay and clerical, proud that
vice had been swept away, pulled down their white
waistcoats and said in loud tones, "Let us render

thanks!" For what? Simply for a coat of white-
wash. But El Paso, unluckily, began to advertise
its virtue far and wide, and so the rest of the
world began to lose interest in the town.

Between the years of 1904 and 1907 it blossomed
out into the small metropolis phase of its career
and the citizens began, hastily, to change their
habits. With as much earnestness as they had
before displayed in enjoying themselves in a free
and unrestrained manner they set about learning
how to live according to the rules which their wives,
who were now taking annual trips back East,
brought home and inserted into the family curric-
ulum. Early in the game the leading business
men took a great fall upward. Regular fellows,
men who had been cowpunchers, had pounded
drills, had weighed out *chile* and *frijoles* by the
pound to nickel customers, and some even who had
driven ice and butcher and grocery wagons and
had learned to know the community through its
back doors, suddenly found that the possession of
virtue made it incumbent upon them to conduct
their business from within the confines of private
offices. This advance into obscurity made another
step imperative. Dignity, like youth, must be
served, and there was one other thing, besides writing letters and signing checks, which, according to
the system now borrowed from Salt Lake City and
Denver, Colo., the financial barons of the town
must do away from prying eyes. That was their
drinking. Public conviviality had become un-

seemly and so these men who had for long, long years been in the habit of calling bartenders by their first names and doing most of their business with one foot on the rail got themselves together and began organizing clubs. For the first time the community made acquaintance with the post-prandial orator and with those other highly decorative municipal improvements, the club president, the club director and the club committeeman. Men who, a short fifteen years before, had been content to sit on their heels and roll their own while they conversed freely and openly with the world, now found themselves confined in a close pasture where etiquette demanded that they smoke perfectos at four bits a throw and associate only with other unfortunates whose genealogies, like their own, were beginning to appear in the new issues of the herd books of Dun and Bradstreet. These poor men now shaved daily, boasted of the cold plunge every morning, changed their clothes by the clock, and began to play golf. This was the end.

OGDEN:

THE UNDERWRITERS OF SALVATION
By
Bernard DeVoto

OGDEN

THE Overland Limited stops at Ogden for fifteen minutes. The tourist, a little dizzy from altitude but grateful for trees after miles of desert, rushes out to change his watch and see a Mormon. He passes through a station that is a deliberate triumph of hideousness and emerges at the foot of Twenty-fifth Street. Beyond him are the peaks, the Wasatch at more than their usual dignity, but in the foreground are only a double row of shacks far gone in disintegration, stretching upward in the direction of the hills. The gutters, advertised as sparkling with mountain water, are choked with offal. The citizenry who move along the sidewalks are habituated to the shanties, but the newcomer, who whether from east or west believes in a decent bluff of progress, is invariably appalled. What manner of folk, he wonders, what kind of Digger Indians, can suffer this daily assault upon the credo of Kiwanis? He thinks of the First National in Kokomo, or the Biltmore in Racine. He shudders. He hurries back to the train, pausing on the way to buy a postcard to which is attached a bag of table salt from Great Salt Lake. That at least is up to date.

Robert Louis Stevenson, the one poet known to have passed through Ogden, faced these same shanties when they had withstood some forty fewer years of drouth. His only contribution to the booster-literature of the city was a note on the Chinese immigrants, who, he observed, displayed a far greater personal cleanliness than the natives.

Lest an Ogden spirit be offended, let me make amends. It is true that the one new building on Twenty-fifth Street since 1900 is the Pullman porters' club. But let us take the tourist blindfolded through the city, past the Cornville Center palaces of the wealthy and the bungalow-warrens of the bourgeoisie, to Ogden Canyon. Past that, still blindfolded against the Keep Kool Kamps and the Dewdrop Inns, to some ridge whence he may see the joists and rafters of a continent, with the city insignificant on the plain. Here he will see Ogden as it is, an oasis, a garden in the desert, with the peaks splendid above it—lines that sweep the eye irresistibly onward, distances and colors that carry the breath with them, the mountains in which the gods of the Utes walked in the cool of the day. For majesty, he will be willing to forget the measles of the street.

Better still, let him arrive on one of the three or four midwinter days when the smoke has drifted westward and left the sky clean. Then, emerging in a heliotrope twilight, he will not see the shanties or the filth. The city is blotted out and there are only ridges deep in snow, saintly and whitened peaks with collars of mist half way down their slopes—mist slowly burning to its core of tourmaline, with sapphires winking at the edge. Night

brings its erasure of hideousness, the good folk ride
homeward in the world's worst trolleys, and presently they are fed and stalled. But almost till the
time they are abed, the eastern peaks, above their
chasubles of mist, are luminous with a garnet flame
that tints the snow against the night. Infinitely
cold, the mist and the darkness; but warm the glow
—a fire burning on the very hearth of heaven.

But do not conclude, because the city is resolute
in shabbiness beneath the peaks, that it is leading
a schism from the faiths of Rotary and Mr. Bok.
Its hideousness, its squalor, are no protest against
The Ladies' Home Journal. Your Ogdenite, instead, sees his city as those dreams come true. He
peoples these streets with the chaos of State and
Madison, lines them with Wrigley Twins, roofs
them with elevateds. To him the Eccles Block is
sixty stories high, and the constable at the corner,
who is flapping a hand at three Fords and an Overland, is waving back six rows abreast of Packards
as far as the traffic towers stretch toward the Chicago River.

Or if not now, at least by to-morrow noon. An
idealist, he sees the illusion in front of the fact of
dirt and mediocrity. A dreamer, he dwells for
ever in the city of his hopes. Besides, when you
come down to it, he asks, turning his back on the
Broom Hotel, what city its size?—etc. Follows a
list of statistics from the Weber Club, of mines and
sugar beets, of warehouses and factories, of jobbers
and railroads and farms. . . . And so on—a small
backwater American city, less immaculate than

most, less energetic, less comfortable, but at one
with its fellows in drowsiness, in safety.

Yet once, even the tourist must remember, once
the frontier marched through Ogden with its char-
iots and its elephants. Once there were demigods
and heroes. Once there was desire and splendor—
something of courage and adventure, something of
battle, life a hot throbbing in the veins. Where
now there are culture clubs and chiropractors, there
was a city shouting its male-ness to the peaks.

For God's sake let us sit upon the ground, and
tell sad stories of the death of Roughnecks.

Into the Mormon hegira of 1845-47 went much
heroism, much genius, much suffering. And yet
the Mormon was a prosaic fellow. His prophet
had been martyred, he himself undertook the desert
for religious freedom, he conquered the wilderness
and, neighboring with the coyote, brought forth a
state. And so on—the recital is familiar. Yet he
did all this without humor and without imagination
—did it with poverty-stricken realism, and above
all with an intangible smugness, a bucolic megalo-
mania, a self-righteousness which assured him that
the Lord God Jehovah, whose hinder parts Moses
and Joseph Smith had seen, watched over all his
businesses and made them sound.

So, for twenty years after their arrival in the
desert, the Latter Day Saints practiced a religion
of thrifty visions. They were such folk as would
be attracted to such a religion. The Church, after
settling all disputes that had racked Christendom

for nineteen centuries, made its own contributions
to theology. It taught a plurality of gods, and,
later, the opportunity for any Mormon to become a
god. It gave its pious swineherds the power to in-
terpret visions, to speak in tongues, to recognize
and cast out devils, to hold conversations with angels. It taught the imminent end of the world;
baptism of the dead; the evil of tobacco and cocoa;
the true nature of ectoplasm; and much other extravagant nonsense. And, of course, it taught polygamy.

So much absurdity has been preached about this
last doctrine, the only one associated with Mormonism in the public mind, that the facts have been
obscured. In Utah polygamy was practiced on an
extensive scale only by Brigham Young, and a
good third of his concubines were purely honorary,
veterans of the hegira, widows of the prophet Joseph, or similarly decrepit alumnae who were
awarded a fraction of his name as a sort of decora-
tion. Only a few of the nobility practiced it at all,
and they did so with not wholly unanimous felicity.
Heber Kimball remarked, with a sincerity that
touches the heart, that if God ever set a curse on
him, it was wives.

The truth is that polygamy was established to
justify certain deplorable impulses of the prophet
Joseph. The vigorous nature of Brigham Young
was adapted to the opportunity thus created, and
these precedents fastened the doctrine on the
Church as the commandment of God, let him follow who might. The institution was breaking down

of its own weight when the national government, by attacking it and rousing the always violent martyr-complex of the Mormons, prolonged it beyond its time. And the reason for its decline, as we shall see, was the one reason whose cogency the Mormon Church has ever recognized. It was an economic mistake. It didn't pay.

For Brigham Young had left Nauvoo with a religion, but had established the State of Deseret with a commercial system. Here they were, in great Salt Lake City during these twenty years, planted on a desert, creating wealth, unhampered by interference. Mr. Werner has recently declared that Brigham's genius for organization and finance entitles him to rank among the greatest minds of his century. At his death his private estate, built up from nothing, was worth three million, and while he was amassing this, he laid the foundations on which the Mormon Church has become the greatest financial power in the intermountain west. Such a man deserves mention with the Belmonts and the Goulds of his time. What Brigham might have done, given stockyards or railroads or steel plants, only those who know most about him are able to imagine.

While he lived Brigham Young was Utah; it follows that, during the first two decades of Salt Lake, he was the city. Fortunately, though the head of the most colorless of American heresies, Brigham was a man of color and power. In the midst of thousands of fanatics who had virtues in abundance but never a jot of imagination, he was one who

easily caught fire. In a creed where any communi-
cant of humor must have laughed himself into apos-
tasy, he had humor—was the one Mormon in all
the history of Mormonism who could laugh.

Above all, he was energy. And the frontier, the
frontier that stirs the heart, was only energy. Day
by day he was driving more surely the stakes of
Zion. Nor did he forget that a prophet deserves
well of the church he is giving an inside track to
heaven. The statutes of the early Territorial legislatures are confined almost exclusively to granting
Brigham Young the timber-rights of this canyon,
the water-rights of that, the sawmill privileges here,
the toll-gate privilege there. He builds houses,
stores, bridges; he sells drygoods, flour, horses; he
directs a theater; he invents apartments; he estab-
lishes a university. When the Territory is surveyed and opened to homesteads, he builds a house
on wheels which his pensioners set down where four
section corners meet, and thus files on government
land by wholesale. He has a finger in the invention
of an alphabet, a purely Mormon language based
on the one spoken in heaven and designed to crowd
out the Gentile tongues on earth. He creates a
Mormon currency, the "wooden money" of later
Gentile sneers, and perhaps the one legal tender of
all history based on the promises of Almighty God.
He publishes a newspaper. He even organizes a
sect of communists, who deed over to him as trus-
tees in trust, the last run of their possessions—deeds
conveying to him chickens and beds and underwear
are on the records of Weber and Salt Lake coun-

ties. And all businesses in the valley have him as
an active or a silent partner,—banks and barrooms,
freight-companies and the mills that manufacture
the holy union-suits of the faithful.

In the midst of all this activity, he is watching
over the souls of his Saints—and is a little troubled
by them. Week by week he is thundering at them
in the Tabernacle, roaring a diapason of wrath and
praise, promising them triumph over the Gentiles
or God-damning them as loafers. For the prophet
had dwelt too long among the Gentiles and had acquired a certain vocabulary. In the "Journal of
Discourses" these sermons are printed today, no
less vigorous for being foul-mouthed, no less productive of piety for being Rabelaisian. Brigham,
simply, could not express himself in other ways.
Here before him was a crowd of Saints, honest men
but so inferior to him that he seemed godlike, mul-
ish and dull, incapable of seeing their own best interests, slow to see anything at all. He would, he
said, infinitely rather kill a man than suffer him to
lose his soul. On occasion, no doubt, he had the
execution performed, but for the most part, swearing sufficed.

For, in these meetings, you must remember, this
bearded man was not merely Brigham Young the
glazier and the millionaire, but was Brigham Young
the seer and revelator, the vicegerent of God, whose
words came down from heaven. Faces, ten thousand at a time, looked up at this little man, and
saw what Christ had seen on the morning of Resur-
rection. . . . This frontier Moses made annual pro-

cessions across his domain. The cavalcade, with
banners and outriders and bodyguard, with Amelia
or perhaps several of the less favored wives, struck
out across the territory. Everywhere children were
scoured and ruffled and drilled to decorum. Young
girls threw flowers—the blossoms of desert plants
or the more cherished hollyhocks of the dooryard
—beneath the wheels of the chariot, and sang their
pious doggerels to this little man, who held one
hand beneath his flatulence and nodded as he fan-
cied God would nod. And old men and women
hobbled back home, happy that they had lived another year to witness the passage of the holy one.

"I'll say we got knives here as well as the boys
in San Pete," he had shouted last Sunday in the
Tabernacle, referring to the irremediable humiliation of a young man who had looked too often on
a maiden designed for his bishop. "Get out your
knives, boys." The Saints hearkened. This was
the prophet of God, the practitioner of polygamy,
telling them that they must not commit adultery.

What Brigham aimed at was a commonwealth of
Saints, wherein all labored for a common end,
where the will of God and the prophets was law,
and where the United States was a foreign power.
For twenty years that was what he achieved. Now
and then, some Saint's voice was raised against the
despotism: there was thunder in the Tabernacle
and a repentance or an exile. Sometimes, it must
be remembered, there was even a corpse. The Mormons of to-day call the Danites a myth; no doubt
they were, but there was Porter Rockwell, there

was Bill Hickman, there was John D. Lee; the
last, deserted by his church after the massacre it
had directed, was shot beside his coffin.

Gentiles came to the valley, forewarned. Sometimes they set up their stores, sometimes offered
merchandise below the prices of the Saints. Soon
neat signboards appeared above the doors of the
faithful—the all-seeing eye of God, sacred in
Mormon symbolism, and above it "Holiness to the
Lord." And men loitered about. A Saint, approaching the Gentile store, felt a tap on his
shoulder. "Brother Brigham favors the Jones establishment," he was told. The Gentile came to
terms. When he didn't, when his tribe increased
so far that it was cutting the ground from under
the Church stores—for a bargain is a bargain even
under the all-seeing eye—Brigham organized a
chain, the Zion's Cooperative Mercantile Institution, which has grown into one of the largest of
the Church's immense properties—and licked the
Gentiles once more.

Governor, judge, and marshal—one by one they
beat out their precedents and sovereignties against
the little bearded man. They had from him smiles
when he wanted to bestow them, but more often
contumely. Cut-throats he called them, and em-
bezzlers, and lick-spittles, and all opprobrious
things. Every Sunday saw him in the Tabernacle
reviling the governor, pouring out on him un-
imaginable abuse. Always he won. Arrested, his
own courts gave him habeas corpus. Denounced,
he replied in kind. Ordered to submit to the

United States, he declared by proclamation that
the territory was his to do with as he willed. Governor gave way to governor, all gladly, some made
laughing-stocks, some disgraced. If their own
foolhardiness did not betray them, it was always
possible to trap them in a trumped-up brothel and
so be rid of them.

In Utah there was no power but Brigham. He
was superior to the United States, not only by
virtue of his agency from God, but actually by
power of arms. So, when the United States sent
an army against him, he outgeneralled the brilliant Albert Sidney Johnston, burned his baggage,
holed him up in winter quarters outside the Territory, and treated as an equal with the United
States. The expedition, which cost the government some seven million dollars, added almost that
much wealth, by auction and the spoils of war,
to the victorious Church. . . . But it was Brigham
at his darkest hour. Boasting to his followers that
he would deliver Zion, he found out what it was
to doubt in secret. The terms of peace allowed
the troops to save their faces by marching through
Salt Lake City and to build a camp some forty
miles beyond.

The Mormons had reason enough for their
hatred of the United States, their prophecies
against it, and their oaths of disaffection. If they
had always met the government with treason, the
government had always betrayed them. The
troops coming through Salt Lake City, who knew
but they might have orders to shoot down all who

got in their way, and generally to lay waste the Jerusalem the Saints had built up with their sweat in the desert? . . .

That day the quickstep echoed through empty streets. No one was in sight, beyond an occasional Gentile waving his hat at a corner. The Mormon women and children were miles away, with their pottery and their blankets, and most of the men were with them. There, too, was Brigham in his chariot. Here and there about the city a Mormon was hidden, ready if need be to light the faggots that were piled behind the doors. Brigham, in valedictory, would bring the city down on the heads of its despoilers.

For once this low-comedy prophet reached dramatic heights. Silent in his chariot, miles away from his Jerusalem, holding up his paunch with an arm, he was planning out his course if the city must be burned. Between the Mormons and the Americans must be war forever—as he had known for years even before the prophet Joseph collapsed over the windowsill at Carthage jail. No longer would he delude himself with hope of peace. He would lead his Church on a second flight, this time to the Canyon of the Colorado, to the badlands where an army could never penetrate. There he would conduct the feud without mercy forevermore—Mormon against American, to the death, while an ounce of powder remained to the faithful.

The tragic heights subsided. The city, of course, was not burned. The wives came back and the Sunday rhapsodies continued. Soon the troops

were called back to a more extensive battlefield
and not even a pretence of authority was kept
over Brigham. As for the deathless feud—that,
too, has been buried by the years, and for the best
of Mormon reasons. It was useless extravagance.
It didn't pay.

The colony at Ogden, thirty-five miles to the
north, had been founded by divine command.
Brigham thumbed through his tithing-lists, selected
those who suited his purposes, and sent them off
to plant another stake of Zion. So, during these
years, Ogden was a scattering of log and adobe
huts, well off the main currents of the frontier.

There is much that is pathetic in the scene of
these earnest Mormons going out to plough their
alkali fields and bring down water from the hills
in the name of God. There is more that is side-
splitting. For, when you meditate on the piety
of this persecuted breed, on this religion that led
thousands across the desert, remember of what in-
gredients that faith was made. Equal parts of
smugness, ignorance, and superstition is the formula. Remember that the God of this Israel was
a person very much in the likeness of Brigham
Young, a fat old man with a bad temper, who used
abominable English, who had begotten mankind
by actual sexual congress with a polygamous
harem of she-gods, and who had undertaken to
deliver the earth into the hands of his anointed.

That is where the earthly humor of Mormonism enters. These simple folk, who ploughed the

desert under and out of the alkali brought forth
bread, these tired, almost dehumanized men were
Chosen People. They walked their furrows by
day and lay down in their shanties by night confident that they were building brick by brick the
new Jerusalem whence some day God and Joseph
Smith and Brigham Young should direct the universe. These fences of cedar were really the
bastions of a new earth. These poplar barns were
the granaries of the Lord, incrusted with pearls.
These trickles of white water—were they not piped
from the four rivers of Paradise?

The frontier passed them by, thirty-five miles
to the southward. Through Salt Lake City went
the pageantry of the American folk-wandering.
Through Salt Lake City streamed the Forty-
Niners, hellbent for California, with their wash-
bowls on their knees. They swarmed their hour
about Brigham's boulevards, bartered their luxuries for staples at extortionate rates, and hurried
on. The Church made a good thing of them, as it
had of the Mexican War before them. In their
wake came the Overland Mail, with its Concord
stages thundering into town behind a dozen mules,
captained by men of a grandeur not to be equalled
off the deck of a Mississippi packet. Followed
the second great mining stampede, to Virginia
City this time, and another wave of violent men,
swaggering their male-ness down avenues dedi-
cated to God and God's dollars. After that, the
pony express, following the stage-route, a venture
that bankrupted its backers but gave the West its

SALT LAKE CITY, UTAH TERRITORY, IN 1857

most colorful legend—a legend of galloping
hoofs, foamy flanks, and the halloo of a rider who
was swallowed up by dust or darkness as soon
as he was seen.

All this energy, all this restlessness and aspira-
tion, streamed through Salt Lake City, under the
eyes of Brigham who saw in it the end of his isola-
tion, perhaps, but also an immediate source of
profit. Ogden it passed by. Ogden was a settlement of pious Mormons who tilled their fields and
obeyed the prophet, who looked at the mountains
but saw the meadows of Jerusalem.

And then word came that the Pacific Railroad
was not disposed to adopt the prophet's suggestion. "Why," said the engineers, "should we
build over an extra divide merely to get to Salt
Lake City when we can follow a water-level route
through Weber Canyon?" And Weber Canyon
debouched a mile or so from Ogden. Then suddenly there was a freight-line from Zion, and a
little later came the surveyors from the east and
from the west. Then a new goldfield, poised
on the present boundary between Idaho and
Wyoming, opened up. An adventurous Gentile
made a trail to it, shortened its line of supplies
two hundred miles, and the first affluence Ogden
had ever seen began.

There were two streets—then three, then four.
Saloons came, bringing progress—bright lights,
tablecloths, store shirts, flowered vests, the etiquette of the Colt. The miners came, and scarlet
women; such women as Ogden had never seen.

Women with laces and silks, with rouge and rice
powder. Women who were all that Mr. Service
has declared their Alaskan sisters to be, but who
brought civilization to this cowpath settlement.
Women who, it may be, troubled the souls of their
Mormon sisters. For Mark Twain, looking im-
partially at the evidence, has said that a man who
married one Mormon woman was a hero and a
man who married a dozen of them was a large-
scale benefactor of the human race.

Strange sights by day in the streets that had
seen nothing more extraordinary than a drove of
pigs. Ox teams by the dozen plodding ahead of
a freighter's wagon with seven-foot wheels and a
bullwhacker snaking his whip above their ears.
Mules singly or in tandem packed with the outfits of prospectors, their owners trudging in their
dust. Gamblers, settlers, bartenders, Mexicans,
Chinks, remittance men. And by night what
sounds! In the saloons, the roar of good men
singing, the fellowship of males, the debate of a
hundred disputants at once, each one an authority.
Above them the seduction of fiddles where the
women consorted with their prey. In the streets,
strayed revelers taking the long way home, the
clop-clop of horses as belated ones arrived, the
click of dice, sometimes the voice of the Colt. . . .
It was a little different from discussions as to the
true nature of Satan's fur, or from the hymns
with which the Mormon dances had begun. Sin
had come to Ogden.

And now descended on Ogden the Hartigans

and the McCarthys and the Flahertys. Through
the mouth of Weber Canyon, racing against its
ten-mile day and the Chinks of the C. P., the
Union Pacific burst like a spring flood. Now
came Hell on Wheels to Mormonry.

Not long did it pause, this mobile terminal, but
never again would righteousness be quite the same.
The Irish roared and sang and hammered, like
happy devils assaulting the earth, and laid their
steel and passed on. On to Corrine they went,
on to Promontory Point, and met the Chinks and
sniped at them from behind ties or seized them
bodily, when the scientific spirit was strong, and
took them apart. Those last eighty miles of railroad building, both companies roaring for land and
fame, were a romancer's dream of strength and
trickery and violence. They ended; dignitaries
came to drive their golden spike; and the Central
Pacific built on into Ogden any way, in the hope
that it could swindle the government of fifty thousand acres more. And the Irishmen all came
back.

For Ogden was now a railroad town. Those
who had swung picks, fought Indians, and sniped
at Chinks, would now undertake to keep the U.
P.'s cars on its tracks. A race of men, these. For
the most part Union veterans, they were old before their youth was done; their arms were like
the girders of the bridges they built; and they,
who had tamed spring rivers and battened rails
across the spine of a continent, were afraid of
neither God nor devil. Still less were they afraid

of men who were anointed to hold converse with both.

It was Porter Rockwell who learned as much soon after the first roundhouse was built at Ogden —Porter Rockwell, mysterious emissary of Brigham, who, if he performed one-tenth of the murders attributed to him had disposed of more Gentiles than Brigham had married wives. Bearded and very hard was Porter Rockwell, a man to set strong men wailing in their dreams, a man who had publicly allowed that the temple union-suit he wore, blessed by Brigham, would turn any bullet ever fired by Gentile. He was strolling down Spring Street one day, newly come from mysteries of retribution, and he was listening to the earth quake in terror of his passing. Appeared now one twisted Flannigan, deplorably gone in drink.

"Are ye Port Rockwell?" the half-size Irishman demanded. The strong right arm of Brigham nodded. "Then by God, y'are the man whose underwear will turn bullets, and I'm called of God to put it to the proof. 'Tis a revelation, y'understand, to speak accordin' to Mormon."

In something less than a second Porter Rockwell was on his knees in Ogden's dust, and had swallowed five inches of steel barrel. For ten minutes the railroader marched round him, dictating enormous obscenities about Brigham Young for his victim to acclaim, and then marched him off down the street for exhibition, the Colt prodding his pants.

Ogden was frontier. From Salt Lake Brigham built his railroad, the Utah Central, to connect with the U.P., and from Ogden northward into his Idaho dominions as the Utah Northern. One landboom after another rocketed city lots. The land agent came, and with him both fortune and bankruptcy. Northward the freighters sent their cavalcades, long files of wagons under the white-gold cloud of dust, creaking of axles and grunt of oxen, oaths and laughter—the strain and vigor of life.

Came too, not only Bret Harte's gambler, but his aristocratic cousin, the confidence man, of derringer and long-tailed coat, who worked the passenger trains and fleeced his traveling companions at faro or sold them mountain peaks or rivers or franchises to build ferries in the desert. The good and the great came, to see what the railroad was doing in the waste places. And now that other symbol of the west began to come,—the cowboy making his long drive northward from Texas, his face hidden in his bandana, his lungs choked with alkali. Ogden was as far west as the Long Trail ever came, as far west as the dionysiac joy of the buckaroo ever set the peaks echoing.

One and all they made their way from bar to bar but ended at the Chapman House. French Pete, other and true name unknown, was the civilizing influence that turned many a man toward the arts. Here is a menu of French Pete's, preserved to this smaller age. Turtle soup, crackers; mountain trout, Columbia river salmon, oysters San Francisco; antelope steak, shoulder of venison, beef Chicago; breasts of sage hen, prairie chicken in cream, quail, mourning doves, Canada goose; southern yams in candy, peas, celery, watercress, potatoes O'Brien; hot biscuits, cornpone; honey, watermelon, peaches and cream. The little slip indicates that one was expected, not to make a choice from this ecstasy, but to down it all from the first to the last. The other side is an equally heroic list; cocktails named after railroad presidents, Indian chiefs, and mining camps; punches, cordials, highballs, fizzes, rickies, Juleps; it ends, "Irish whiskey, fifteen cents a glass." And one line reads, "Champagne: California, $1.00. Imported, $2.00." A pint? No, a half-gallon.

To the Chapman House came the mining and railroad millionaires, the English cattle-barons, actors and singers making continental tours, and more than one princeling from Graustark or beyond. The register, if it could be recovered, would be a miniature history of the frontier. Perhaps most curious of its names would be the curtly signed "Bill." This was Rattlesnake Bill, who came for some weeks twice or thrice a year, to eat the savories of French Pete, and to sit for hours on the upper veranda, smoking, chatting, looking down at Fifth Street or out at the shadows deepening on the peaks.

Innumerable legends cluster about this man of the white sombrero above the long black curls. No one ever ventured to ask his name. No one knew

whence came the money that clad and housed him
so magnificently. One heard that he was a Mason
sent to murder Mormons, that he owned a secret
bonanza surpassing the Comstock Lode, that he
was successively all the desperadoes who plun-
dered the mines and the mail, that he was the
illegitimate son of a British prince and once a
month received an order on the royal exchequer.
He had killed, one understood, his dozen; he had
led men on desperate piracies beyond the hills; he
had said to men in New York, in China, or in
London, "Do this," and it was done.

But there he sat, smoking cigars that were never
bought in Ogden, telling stories to the Chapman
children, and bowing to men and women who
counted his nod an accolade. Once a year he contributed to Catholic, Mormon and Protestant
Churches; and at Christmas time all railroad men
on duty and all wayfarers fed at his expense on
French Pete's cooking. He died one night in the
Chapman House, of an apoplexy. No papers
were found in his buffalo trunk. But there were
books there: Childe Harold, a Shakespeare, several originals of Voltaire, and a volume of strange
devices which pious Saints believed to be the original of the Book of Mormon, which would have
made Bill the angel Moroni. But it proved to be
only a sixteenth century Odyssey, whose *ex libris*
had been obliterated.

Near the Chapman House was Gentile Kate's
brothel, incomparably the leader of its kind. Kate
was herself a respected part of the business life

of the town, a speculator in real estate, the most
liberal customer of the stores; she was, too, an
unofficial great lady. When a railroad dignitary
or a visiting Cabinet member was to be banqueted,
she was always bidden to provide conversation and
fine raiment above the reach of Ogden. No one
was ever swindled at her establishment; no one
was ever disorderly there, twice. A person of
dignity was Gentile Kate, and of more than a
little wit. But her annoyance was Mormons—
perhaps because she disliked their colorlessness,
perhaps because she felt that their multiple marriages were sabotage against her profession, perhaps because she had knowledge of certain patri-
archs and bishops who, by day, denounced her in
their meeting-houses. Doing almost a bank's business in loans and mortgages, she never lent a
penny to a Mormon; and the one unladylike expression in her vocabulary coupled a vivid gene-
alogy with the name of Joseph Smith.

Early in her career, Brigham Young died of
overeating, and soon there was an auction of his
effects. Of late years he had taken to parading
the streets of Salt Lake in a new carriage—a
barouche made for him in the East. One sees the
picture: Brigham at his portliest, at his most be-
nignant, leaning back in the wine-colored cushions, one arm bracing his paunch, his eyes stray-
ing over the multitudes who uncovered and bowed
their heads as the right hand of God went by. An
equipage of splendor, behind gray stallions, on
one side the all-seeing eye, carved and glistening,

on the other side the beehive of Deseret, and on
the rear the angel Moroni ascending to heaven
from audience with Joseph Smith. But only a
carriage, after all.

The Utah Central, one day, bore it up to Ogden. Next day, behind the same gray stallions,
bearing the same insignia of Mormonry, it rolled
up and down the streets of Ogden, and haughty
in its cushions was Gentile Kate.

Meanwhile, following the Irish, other people
were settling in Ogden, putting up their stores,
shipping their freight to the multitudes of little
towns that had germinated in the railroads' wake.
Much money was being made in Ogden—and this,
as it was Gentile money, gravelled the Mormon's
souls. Now begins the last protracted struggle
between the faithful and the damned. As always,
it gave the Mormon more than his native color.
Unmolested, he is only a fanatic worshiping outrageous gods; but fighting the Gentile, he is laved
with all the high-lights of martyrdom and sanctity
and desperation. Brigham Young was dead, but
behind the figureheads of the presidency was
George Q. Cannon, who was scarcely less a general.

Politics had served the Church well in Illinois;
perhaps the Mormon ability to cast ten thousand
votes as one might help out now. For a dozen
years the battle waged unequally—centered, of
course, in Ogden where alone the Gentiles might
make a stand. The town began to glow. Its

somnolent avenues to-day bear no hint that they have witnessed emotions no less intense than those that followed Bloody Mary about her realm. They were for the most part bloodless, but were no less bitter; only, the Irish kept them on the comic side. Your Mormon, battling at Armageddon for his dollar, is no light-minded man; he regards levity as the sin against the Holy Ghost; his god, as the god of this world, centers his interest in cash, wherefore to be else than solemn is to risk hell. But the Irish, who had created and obliterated the frontier, were less awed.

A merry decade it was, these ten years of the People's Party and the Liberal Party—ten years of plot and counterplot, of stuffed ballot boxes and bribed judges, of scandals built to order and set off at the right moment; of broken heads, of oratory and defiance. From Mormon pulpits streamed curses that had for their model the chapters of Deuteronomy which raise cursing to an art. From Irish bar-rooms streamed the laughter of men. Sometimes a Gentile Machiavelli was set upon by night in an alley and his head was bashed. Sometimes one was bought outright or another caught with the goods. In the last case he would be tried by Mormon jury before a Mormon judge, with his comrades—who wasted no sympathy on a man who could get caught—swearing him into centuries of prison.

Sometimes a madness would come upon the Irish, and they would go out for entertainment. Bishop Jones, hurrying to priesthood meeting,

would find himself captive to a dozen brawlers
who would, perhaps, drag him to the new steam
laundry, strip him, and immerse him in a vat of
soap with lewd parodies of the Temple ordinances.
Did he believe Brigham Young had taken to wife
Semiramis and Cleopatra and the Queen of
Sheba?. Down with him into the suds! Did he
expect to beget souls in heaven? Let the soap
cover him! And so on till the bishop, recanting
Mormonism, precept by precept, emerged a bishop
of the black mass.

They went forth to battle, these Irish, but they
always died. Till one November the auguries
pointed the other way and the Irish swaggered
down the middle of the streets. Election day saw
two machines perfected. One by one, in the outlying districts where no Gentiles lived, the Mormons filed in, voting for themselves, for their
wives, their children, their great grandparents, and
the legions they had taken to wife in celestial marriage. A Gentile election-judge nodded jovially
and called them by their first names. All day long
till the polls closed. Then, out of nowhere, came
rigs galloping; hard men descended on the polls,
lifted the ballot box, and disappeared with the
Gentile judge. Down the Weber and Ogden
rivers flowed streams of ballots sanctified by the
Lord's chosen.

Word had reached the Liberal headquarters
that special trains had come up from Salt Lake
City and that the Mormons were voting all the
names on the tombstones. Headquarters grinned

and consulted watches. A special arrived from as
far north as the Idaho line—and northward there
were only Mormons. The upper floor of the city
hall filled with a reserve to be called into action
ten minutes before the polls closed. A Gentile
leader made to go up the stairs. No less a man
than Porter Rockwell, now aging, and soon to
die, tapped him on the shoulder.

"My orders," Porter said, "is to shoot anybody
that goes up them stairs."

The Gentile nodded and beckoned two deputy
marshals who happened, very casually, to be
standing nearby. "Your orders," he informed
them, "is to shoot anybody that comes down them
stairs."

An hour before the polls closed all the locomotives in the railroad yards began to whistle. Two
specials roared in from Echo, Wasatch, Evanston, and points east. How many Irish clambered
down from cars and roofs and tenders history
does not estimate. But they streamed uptown and
began to vote. They voted the payrolls of the
U.P., the registers of the Chapman House and
the Broom Hotel, the tax-lists of Evanston, and
every other document that bore names. Then, re-
versing first and last names, they voted again. . . .

That night the planets knew that Gentile Ogden was delivered from the oppressor's heel. How
much firework was burned, how much firewater
drunk, it is a melancholy business to calculate.
The peaks gave back shriekings until dawn. And
at dawn a cowboy who had been making his first

visit to Ogden was discovered setting up a sign
on a hill some miles from the city.

"Ogden City," the sign read. "Ogden City.
Hotter than Hell and the Hottest Place This
Side of Hell."

About this time, too, the Mormons achieved
their last moment of dignity. Persistently they
had agitated Statehood, to remove the congres-
sional supervision exercised under the Territory.
Persistently their hamstringing of governors and
their practice of polygamy had stood in their way.
The Liberal victory pricked them to greater efforts, but coincidently, the propaganda of Gentile
sects became effective and the Edmunds-Tucker
bill, the first anti-polygamy measure with teeth,
passed Congress. At once the Mormons found
themselves helpless, once more martyrs, once more
hunted, once more without civil rights. Church
property was confiscated, all who practiced polygamy were placed without the law, and all who
would not disavow it were disfranchised. The
government had them where the hair was short.

For a moment, then, the familiar Mormon
frenzy of martyrdom. Mass-meetings of women
all over the Territory resolved their ardor for
polygamy—a phenomenon to be explained not so
much by a woman's preference for one-tenth of a
superior man to a whole lout, as by the priesthood's Mohammedan domination over its women.
Mormon leaders, with a price on their heads, disappeared into the desert. In Ogden there was
secret traffic by night, riders going out from son

in control to father in hiding, other riders following them to head off pursuit. The pulpits flamed with their old-time hatred of the United States.

A moment of tragedy, a moment when God seemed to be testing his chosen with the fire that had tried their fathers, a moment that seemed bound to repeat the catastrophe of Nauvoo, when the Church, without leaders, money or supplies, was driven out to face the desert. Only this time there was not even a desert; Israel could not isolate itself from Babylon, but must be scattered piecemeal and destroyed, all for the purest motive man ever defended, for religious faith. So there was peering into darkness, heartbreak, resolution, and despair. . . . The last downstage tableau of the Saints.

But only for a moment. The stuff of Mormonry had grown both weaker and wiser. Remember Brigham, fulminating his defiance of the government, stationing men with torches in his forsaken city, resolved to lead his Church to the Canyon of the Colorado and there fight the United States unto the end. Mormonry had changed: it could now contemplate the destruction of a dogma without shudders, but the loss of property was something else. It recalled that when Brigham had opposed the Gentiles with force he had often been menaced and sometimes licked, whereas no one in history had ever beaten him in a business deal. . . .

It is recorded that those in authority who

favored the trial by battle were looked on by the rest with a certain wild impatience, as men who had not penetrated the symbolism of God's truth. So presently polygamy was repealed, not by revelation but by declaration of inexpediency, and except for old fogies tottering with their harems to the grave, it is now obsolete.

It is a doctrine still, now made intricate with years of rationalization, but it is taught the young Saints as an ordinance to be practiced hereafter in those days to come when all men are made perfect, when the Saints dwell like gods with their grandfathers and their grandsons, when Brigham and Joseph come back with their wives and take their proper stations somewhere between the first and second members of the Trinity. The latest President of Israel treats those suspected of believing too currently in plural marriage with the ferocity his predecessors reserved for rival revelations. He is right. Any effort to bring polygamy from the hereafter to the now is bad business. It doesn't pay. And, in the end, for Mormonry, there is no other test for truth.

So vanished the last energy of Utah, of Salt Lake City and of Ogden. Why should Israel longer fight Gentiles with politics? Why should it longer retain beliefs which meant a money loss? Why should it indulge itself with martyrdom, the most extravagant of all waste? After all, the father's house held many mansions and the victory promised the Saints could be worked out in the most formidable of them, the counting-house.

And so it was. Mormon organization, a priesthood whose function is ambivalent, a communistic system directed by a tight oligarchy, the religious force harnessed to economic machines—all these have, in thirty years, brought Israel into its kingdom. Your Mormon dwells in peace and brotherly love with his Gentile neighbor, for intolerance and warfare lost money—they didn't pay. He fights no more political or social battles—they wasted money in the old days. In 1917, instead of Brigham's vilification of the government as of 1861, and his prayers for the success of the South, the Church oversubscribed its Liberty Loan quotas and outdid New England in hatred of the Teuton. For patriotism pays.

The Mormon has done well. There are no Mormon poor. The Church looks after its own. The "peculiar people" have a stranglehold on the wealth of the intermountain region. God's promises have been certified. The underwriters of salvation have made good. Even the religion tends toward Rotary: you must dig through many layers of rationalism and defence before you get at the awkward gods, the taboos, and the ignorance at the core. For color of history or of person, for individuality and all such strange, un-Mormon impulses—these, too, do not pay.

That is why the tourist, singling out his Mormon bishop for identification, is most likely to pick out the high-church rector of St. Luke's. That is why the real Mormon bishop looks like a

bank-director; he is one. That is why to-day a
Mormon is indistinguishable from a Gentile in
Ogden. The Church of Jesus Christ of Latter
Day Saints has come into its own; it has inherited
the promised land, the promised power, the promised glory. It has won its battle; it has tamed
its cities; it has delivered its enemies into slavery.
In all things. . . . Only, of course, victory carries with it its own sequelæ. Mormonry, let it be
said, once more, is a religion of this earth, a deifi-
cation of produce and merchandise and high interest. And naturally it has reaped in kind. The
Ogden of to-day, we have noticed, is hideous, intolerably. The life that goes on behind its dingy
walls is no less so. No less so in Salt Lake City
or in the uttermost parts of the State.

The bishop of an Ogden ward—"ward" is the
appropriate Mormon term for parish—was presenting to his church a picture which one of his
flock had painted to the glory of his people. Save
for the halo round Brigham's head, the smear
might have been torn from a billboard advertising
Camels. And wholesome awe was in that bishop's
voice.

"Brother Sorenson tells me," said Bishop Jor-
genson, "that the materials in this painting cost
him less than six dollars. If he had not wanted to
give it over to the Church, he could have sold it
for fifty dollars. That, my brethren, is how it
pays to get an education for the glory of your
Church." The congregation sang its hymn of
praise. A young priest in the back row sighed,

and surreptitiously putting on his shoes went to the table to bless and distribute the sacrament. . . .

The mountains all about, one would think, ought to bring something of splendor into the lives of those who live among them, something of poignancy, of beauty. Here about the Chosen People are extravagance and excess of beauty— why, then, has it never worked its way into their hearts? Well, the Church was first enlisted and has ever since been increased from the bankrupt fringe, from the very dregs of foreign and domestic society. Neither artists nor their patrons flourish among such folk. And then, a man who can believe in the pathological god of Joseph Smith and who must worship him after the mercantile manner of Brigham Young, such a man has little understanding of beauty or refinement and no patience with them. They do not pay.

Talent, by biological aberration, does sometimes arise here in Ogden. A child is born with a voice, with a gift for the stage, the violin, or the brush. The Church is kind to him. However modest his circumstances, he is sent to conservatories or to dramatic schools or wherever else training may be had for him. And in due time he is brought back to drill the faithful in singing "O, My Father," or to teach their children how to paint sago lilies in their sketches of the prophet Joseph talking to the angel Moroni. I do not deny that the Mormons have an art. They have the most appalling art this side of the Australian bush (where they now proselyte), and it is practiced for the glory of the

Church as was the art that reared the cathedrals of France. Cooperative competition for the glory of the Church and the profit of its rulers is the Mormon formula. So the child who can recite "The Village Blacksmith" gets a point for his ward in the monthly standing; his sister, by setting a stanza of Eliza Snow's doggerel to something resembling music, may get five points for the ward, thereby equalling Annie Christopherson, of the next ward, who during the week invented a new way of making cake without eggs.

And, asks the bishop, is there any other worthy kind of art? Does any other art make us better Mormons? Does it make us more efficient? Does it add to the stature of the Church?

So the Mormons have dwelt their eighty years among the mountains and never seen them. And, because they have won their battle, they have kept the Gentiles from seeing them as well. . . . Down the streets of Ogden to-day go the Mormon Buicks and the Gentile Fords, equally intent on the matter at hand. No dominant energy is apparent. The frontier is buried deep beneath this crumbling asphalt. By day or night there is no dust of mule teams, no roar of miners' chorus or shout of Irish going forth against the Chink or the Mormon. Even the transient color of the tourist flees away.

Why not? Since frontiers must fall Ogden could not be Hell on Wheels for ever. Not even its ghosts will walk for it but emigrate westward to Hollywood where at times they lift another squalid art to moments of insight. And if Ogden is not an American city, if it will not bustle or erupt, if it is dingy and penurious and sleeping— why, for that too it has a recompense. It is an outpost of the New Jerusalem, concentrated on the things that pay.

Wherefore some day all cities will bend their heads in its direction while the skies open to sudden thunder and St. Brigham and St. Joseph Smith Jun., sharing between them Helen of Troy and all dead, aphrodisiac ladies, come down to chain the devil and populate the earth with Mormon robots.

DENVER:

WASHED WHITER'N SNOW
By
George Looms

DENVER

VIRTUE being a symbol may occasionally be fashioned out of flimsy material. Civic virtue differs in no wise in this respect from individual virtue. Its tailor is the press agent and his work has been known to be undependable. Sometimes he knowingly works with shoddy.

This brief is for the virtue of Denver, Colorado. And disregarding the straight and narrow styles of repute which her tailormen have fashioned for her it may be interesting to catch a surreptitious glimpse of her nude civic body even at a risk of being caught by a Grundy and subsequently disgraced. Such a glimpse can never be enjoyed with sufficient leisure, for one can never know when some one hundred per cent American may come up behind and catch him by the scruff of his neck and perform the conventional practice upon his nether portion. However, no risk, no profit, and little pleasure.

Denver was born on two sides of Cherry Creek in 1858. For over a year she enjoyed two names and two identities; she was both Auraria and Denver City. Accounts differ as to who her natural father was, hence it might appear that she was born out of wedlock.

The deduction is probably correct. Cities are

legitimately born of an idea out of a situation. In
the case of Denver the idea was a fake, the situation a jade and the union surreptitious. The idea
was that there was enough gold in Cherry Creek
to. warrant a national pilgrimage. The situation
was a great body of flat prairie infested with tum-
ble weed, prairie dogs and cactus plants. The as-
signation was with malicious intent and from the
union came a city that has since grown to a fine
and lusty maturity of nearly three hundred thousand souls.

But for nearly a year it seemed that the puny
and unwanted offspring would succumb to malnu-
trition. Mother situation was dry as dry and she
had been betrayed by a lover who had no visible
means of support. The washings of gold in Cherry
Creek were so meagre that they did not yield the
visiting miner more than sixty or seventy cents a
day at the maximum. So in the latter part of
1858 and in the early weeks of 1859 there they
were, twin cities nursing at the public font and
getting no nourishment to speak of. But on May
the sixth, 1859, to use the same figure, a foster
father was found for the infant civic idea in the
guise of a very rich vein of rotten quartz up in
Gregory Gulch about thirty miles to the northwest and the family problem was solved.

Men came across the plains, six, seven and eight
hundred miles to aid the new idea and also to line
their pockets. They came with attendant hard-
ship. They came from less romantic environments
but they brought the imprint of rigid social order.

In the main the Ten Commandments had been popular with them. But the physical demands of the trip proved to be so tremendous that the more ephemeral notions managed to dissipate and upon arrival it was found that only the more rugged symbols of righteous conduct had survived. Articles six and eight of the Mosaic code were the only ones to reach Cherry Creek in any sort of working condition to speak of. Forbidding manslaughter and larceny as they do they form the binder of all known types of social mixture. They were at once incorporated into and strengthened by an immediate practice.

Men came to Denver in those years at great hazard to their skins. The two largest ideas on their horizons were to keep those skins whole and accumulate wealth. The latter had been the initial urge; the former had acquired stature through the austerity of that six hundred mile trek across the plains. Hence, to the pioneer, the two unspeakable crimes in his decalogue were to kill him or to deprive him of his vision.

Denver in those days was a part of Kansas Territory, but Kansas was not so vigorous then as now and her long arm did not reach to her extremities to alleviate any paltry itch. So Auraria and Denver City attended to such irritations locally. And they did so with thoroughness and dispatch.

The first record of community enterprise seems to be in connection with one Moses Young, Esquire, whose early personal history is incomplete.

On March 13th. Young met William West on the mountain side of Cherry Creek between Larimer and Market Streets and emptied fifteen buckshot from his weapon into West's body for no good civic reason. He was caught the next day, not having travelled far; tried by a gentlemen's court and found guilty. The same gentlemen hanged him forty-eight hours later with the same sense of detachment.

On March 30th, John Rooker and Jack O'Neil agreed to settle a difference of opinion in a dark room with bowie knives. The news of the intended affray was circulated and much interest was aroused. But at the eleventh hour Rooker developed a weak stomach and O'Neil indulged in the obvious repartee at his expense. It stirred Rooker to desperation, for the assault upon his good name involved to some extent the repute of his immediate progenitors. Westerners always have been particularly sensitive to this type of criticism; so when the two men met shortly thereafter in a popular drinking resort Rooker shot O'Neil dead. Inasmuch as the act did not violate the civic expectations, it having been advertized that one life at least should forfeit by previous legal contract, Rooker was not thought to have done wrong and was duly acquitted.

John Stoefel, a Hungarian, had followed a brother-in-law, Thomas Biencroff, across six hundred miles of prairie with the purpose of acquiring title to the latter's earthly plunder which, judged by present standards, was hardly worth the trip.

On April 7th., 1859, Stoefel slew Biencroff with an ax messily and injudiciously, injudiciously in that he made no effort to destroy the clews. Perhaps he was overconfident and did not realize the solidity of the apparently loose social mixture of Denver City. On April 7th came the murder. On April 7th Stoefel was apprehended. On April 7th he received a trial by his peers. And on April 7th he was hanged from a cottonwood tree on Cherry Creek, thereby establishing a record and a precedent.

He stood in a wagon with a minister and an executioner, the latter known in Denver City as "Long Tom." There was a short prayer in which the minister and "Long Tom" took part, both kneeling. Stoefel stood, numbed. Upon arising, "Long Tom" kicked Stoefel in the ribs and asked him if he didn't know better than to act like a heathen. The two ends of the rope were conventionally fastened: one to the tree and the other to Stoefel's neck. Then they drove the wagon away and Stoefel became a tradition.

A week later the community slipped into lax practice. A man named Scudder shot and killed a carpenter named Captain Bassett. For some reason he was allowed to escape. A saw-mill was stolen from a steamboat on the Missouri and carted to Denver, set up and started. A few months later the original owner came upon it on Blake Street, hard to work. He proved ownership and the luckless purchaser had to turn it over. The unscrupulous "middle-man," the scorner of titles, was never apprehended. The episode was a sobering one to the young city.

Thomas Clemo, "Chuck-a-luck" Todd and William Karl stole a wagon-load of turkeys and sold them at a nice profit. They were not as careful to keep their anonymity as the saw-mill pilferer. They strapped on their guns, stated that they were the most important men in the community and ordered all disputants to the claim in off the streets. Their ranks were quickly augmented by admirers whose reputations in subsequent histories seem to have been sullied by the charge of opportunism.

One of these last, a Mr. P. M. McCarthy, carried away by his new-found enthusiasm, fired at one W. H. Middaugh as the latter stood in the doorway of the Vasquez House, a hostelry at Eleventh and Ferry Streets. The bullet missed its mark and Mr. Middaugh went into the hotel. Then a Mr. Harvey, another convert to the new individualism, fired at the same Middaugh through a window of the hotel, thus violating an established privacy. The citizenry felt that this last gesture was quite too profane and called out the militia for drill. The militia patrolled the town that night in its own way. McCarthy, still restless and dissatisfied, approached one of the amateur sentries and made motions at him with a bowie knife. But the sentry happened to make up for his lack of border technique with a civic enthusiasm and he bashed in McCarthy's skull with his rifle barrel. Thereupon Harvey, who had

followed McCarthy out of a native curiosity felt
called upon to assert his manliness and drew his
revolver. The second relief arrived at this junc-
ture and Harvey's temper cooled.

The next morning, the citizens issued an order
that the Todd-Harvey crowd leave the city—Mc-
Carthy having succumbed to his injury. But such
enterprises are usually marked by a general raising of the community pulse and thereupon one
George Steele who lived across the river, came
riding through the streets anathematizing the town
in no uncertain language. He was not able to
make his language stick, however, for a dozen
militiamen likewise roused rode forth to meet him
causing him to ride back into the West from
whence he came. There was peace in town for six
weeks thereafter.

Lest any misapprehension develop that the taking of life was the only practice to call out a
community expression of disapproval, a digression
from the chronology of this outline is necessary.
One of the first malpractices engaged in Denver
was the practice of "land-jumping." There being
no courts of record on the ground, possession was
even more than nine points in the law. Should a
claimant find it necessary to leave his mining
claim or his town plot over night he was apt to
find it occupied on the morrow by some sort of
emergency shack bristling with rifles and defiance.
Two human agents were usually to be found besides.

An incorporated "town company" made a busi-

ness of acquiring assets in this fashion. Messrs.
W. H. Parkinson, Thompson and Mickey were
the executive officers of the company and their
aggressive policy soon made them unpopular. A
series of town meetings was held and the situation
discussed. Messrs. Parkinson, Thompson and
Mickey would build sheet-iron shacks, stock them
with an arsenal of forty to fifty rifles, and keep a
vigilant night and day watch. Hence the town
committee saw fit to approach its problem ver-
bally. Ostensibly the members of the company
were on cordial terms with the citizens of the town,
speaking pleasantly at all casual street encounters
but one day a Major R. B. Bradford forgot himself so far as to speak warmly and adversely of
the practices of Mr. Parkinson, which so incensed
the latter that when the two gentlemen passed on
the street the next day, he, Parkinson, fired three
revolver shots at the major at close range—and
missed him every time. This blatant show of in-
capacity did much to crystallize public sentiment
and the citizens thereupon passed an ordinance
that the landjumpers be reimbursed for their pains
and trouble and shown the door of the city. Land-
jumping became taboo and no further record of
its practice in Denver is known.

To resume:

Marcus Gredler and Jacob Roeder had pooled
their resources and efforts in a mining venture and
were in camp near the mouth of Bear Creek
Canon, south-west of Denver a few miles. For
some reason Gredler became incensed with his

partner and cut off his head with an ax on June 12th., 1859. Now it may seem by the mere editorial selection of these episodic landmarks that the new community was nothing if not vigilant. Whether they managed to catch every lawbreaker or not is not determinable for the acts of those who may have managed to get away may have been buried in an editorial silence. But it is recorded that the upholders of the weal caught Marcus Gredler. They tried him in Apollo Hall on June 13th. And on June 15th they hung him from a tailor-made scaffold at the intersection of Cherry Creek and Curtis Street.

The civic spirit was not allowed to abate for long. William T. Hadley, a wagon boss, lent emphasis to his verbal discipline of an employee with a butcher knife. The employee died. On June 24th Hadley was tried by a people's tribunal under the judicial leadership of Mr. William Person. The evidence was adduced in the presence of five hundred citizens. The judge put the decision up to a vote. The prisoner lost the case by four hundred and nine votes to one. He accepted the verdict with a marvellous calm and as a reward for his "he-manly" deportment was granted two days' respite in which to write to his family and settle his estate. On June 26th he was given into the custody of a voluntary hanging committee and on that night he managed to escape. Much bitter feeling developed inasmuch as collusion was charged. Hadley was never again apprehended though a party of immigrants coming into Denver met him far down the Platte and reported that he had made mention of his adventures in a light and airy vein.

The chronicle does not vary materially. Charles Harrison, a bad man, shot and killed a negro by the name of Stark in Cibola Hall because the latter had the presumption to suggest that he take a part in Harrison's poker game. Stark was a free "nigger," having paid for his freedom out of his own pocket. As events developed his new-found self-reliance proved his social undoing. Harrison was not arrested nor brought to trial, the present-accepted symbols of race equality not having been fully established in the new town.

Cibola Hall thus became the dramatic background for many a subsequent passing. Six days later James A. Gordon, who was part owner of the hall, shot down Frank O'Neill, who was a young man of ambition and proprietor of a house of ill repute on Arapahoe Street. O'Neill recovered and returned to his labors. On July 20th Gordon, out gunning for competitors, shot twice at another resort keeper known as Big Phil. Big Phil was considered to be a civic liability and so escaped unharmed through flight.

Gordon whose blood had not quite cooled then went to the Louisiana Saloon and, finding there a young German immigrant by the name of John Gantz, proceeded to vent his exuberance upon him. The latter being a stranger in Denver and pleasantly desirous of offending none of its influential citizens put up no resistance to Gordon's rough behavior. Gordon threw Gantz to the floor. Gantz got up and left the saloon. Gordon followed him and dragged him back into the centre of an admiring audience where he knocked the young visitor flat. One always subjects oneself to a risk of discomfort and inconvenience in visiting any strange community and of course this was a recognized fact in 1859. Hence no one interfered.

Gordon thereupon lost all sense of civic responsibility—so say some chroniclers. Others merely suggest that he was actuated by a higher purpose, namely that of keeping the mines safe for one hundred per cent American democracy. Which is partisan of them. He straddled the chest of the prostrate Gantz and in playful fashion put a pistol to his head, holding him steady by the hair. Gantz still "took the joke," the onlookers standing back in admiring acquiescence. It will be seen that "yes men" are not an exclusive product of the twentieth century. But Gantz was carrying his geniality too far. So Gordon snapped his pistol. He snapped it three times. There was a silence in the place and Gantz had established a reputation for watchful waiting. Gordon snapped the trigger once more. On the fourth time the gun went off and the amiable brains of Mr. Gantz were strewed upon the floor.

The occupants of the saloon then behaved conventionally. Up to the third snapping Gordon had merely been playing. The accidental discharge of the loaded gun put him in another class.

He had gone too far. So when he ran out of the saloon they ran after him—not too quickly—but with reasonable dispatch. He escaped to Fort Lupton. He was followed there by a party of gentlemen who had determined to make an example of him.

The next day they approached the fort on horseback and Gordon spying them from a distance fled the post on his horse. Then began a chase which might qualify for a Tom Mix or "Hoot" Gibson thriller. For ten miles three men pursued one man, all four men exchanging the usual amenities, shooting from the hip. Gordon's horse went down but somehow he managed to get away. It was learned later that he had fled to Indian Territory.

Then W. H. Middaugh, who has featured as a target earlier in this chronicle, volunteered to follow him and bring him back to justice. Middaugh seems to have been a man with a robust stomach, a man worthy of the stature of a symbol. Perhaps he lacked the proper press connections or fell somewhere short in the necessary picturesque personal equation, so his image graces no drinking fount nor public park esplanade in Denver to-day, thoroughly as his career deserves it. He followed Gordon, who was accustomed to standing alone against many and making them like it, to the fastnesses of Coffey County, Kansas, and there made him captive on September 28th. He travelled over three thousand miles to do so and when he returned to Denver a public

purse was raised and his expenses paid in full by
a grateful populace.

For by this time Gordon, free and on the world,
was a smirch on the symbol of law and order
which was beginning to vie with the climate in
importance. Gordon was brought to Denver in
chains, a great trace chain about his waist and
shackles on his wrists and ankles. A ceremony
was made of his trial for it was a symbolical victory. At Sixteenth and Wazee Streets a people's
court was called. The day was October 2nd. The
jury brought in a prompt verdict of wilful murder. Thereupon the prisoner was brought to the
judge's seat, a balcony of Nelson Sergeant's
"Tremont House."

The judge stood on the balcony. Three thousand people stood in the street. Before them and
below the judge, bareheaded and heavily shackled,
stood Gordon, the killer. Beside his swart and
stolid captor he stood with head averted. The
judge put the question to the crowd: "What is
your pleasure?" There was a great roar the import of which was unambiguous. So His Honor
delivered sentence and civic virtue recessed for
the day.

On October the sixth Gordon was hanged from
a scaffold on the east bank of Cherry Creek near
Fourteenth and Arapahoe Streets. He had re-
quested that his captor, Mr. Middaugh, act as his
executioner. Middaugh, who apparently failed in
no civic duty, performed the office with credit.
Three years later he himself was shot down by an

unknown party in Julesburg. It has always seemed that the highly developed social instinct is not a convenient attribute outside a highly developed social environment.

It is thus to be seen that 1859 was not a dull year in the spraddling town. In 1860 there was some trouble with an organized band of horse-thieves. In the early summer of that year twenty-six horses were stolen from Bradley's Ranch, thirty-three from Mallory's Ranch and forty-seven from a man named Kershaw. In September the indignant owners found a "poor white" known as "Black Hawk" with a number of the stolen animals. He could not give them a reasonable explanation so they brought him to the new city and confined him in the cellar of the Cherokee House at Fifteenth and Blake Streets. It was noised about that a secret tribunal would undertake to adjudicate his case. It is certain that on the next night somebody took him out of his cellar room and hanged him from a cottonwood tree on Cherry Creek.

The tradition then goes on to state that in his mental upset and worry he confessed his guilt and implicated some prominent Denver citizens, the implication being that the enterprise had been carefully planned by a band of intelligent horse-thieves in high circles, a sort of horse-thief trust with a great territory extending from Wisconsin to Colorado. There was some resultant nervousness in town, for the new social fabric seemed to be weakening. The next night, which happened to be Monday, an agreeable, stoutish gentleman by the name of John Shear, well known and popular in local convivial circles, was taken from his room in the Vasquez House and hanged to another cottonwood tree on the banks of the Platte. Denver at that became distinctly jumpy and nervous. Whom was one to trust? Two white men had been hung without the usual amenities, with no pressagenting whatever. One of them, Shear, had been a Denver councilman under the old Jefferson Territory Charter. And he had bought a multitude of Denverites a lot of good liquor over various bars.

There was something sinister in his taking off. Despite its homely aspects the home of justice in the people's courts had been acquiring a tradition. And this new practice was violating that tradition. Justice, like other symbols, has no right to change its habitation unceremoniously.

But the excitement was not to abate abruptly. On the night of Shear's silent abduction a certain Judge A. C. Ford left town very quietly. He had had an agreeable reputation in Denver, was thought to be one of Denver's better citizens and was not without a certain suavity, dignity, and social grace. The only question that could be levelled at his character was that he had in his time defended a number of very questionable characters. But what successful lawyer has not? Ford left Denver on the night of September the third on a Missouri River stage. About seven miles east, near the present township of Montclair, the stage was halted by four quiet, well-mannered men. They called for Ford, who stepped out upon the ground without a word. They caused him to mount one of their horses and then told the coach to proceed. The occupants caught a final glimpse of them, riding slowly away around a hillock. About a mile from the trail the four horsemen dismounted and told Ford to dismount. It appears that "the judge" was admirably cool throughout the whole ordeal. There, in a little slough, in a patch of tall grass, they shot him, ensemble-fashion, to avoid any trace of personal animosity.

A few days later the driver of a stage-coach found the body and brought it to Denver. Ford's fine gold watch which he was known to possess was missing. At once questions were asked. A certain low character had left Denver a day or two previously, it was recollected, so a quiet little search party was at once dispatched. They found the fugitive with Ford's watch in El Paso, Texas. They brought the watch back to Denver and turned it over to Ford's widow with suitable regrets. Justice is justice and a man may not take personal advantage of its decrees.

There is a lot of loose talk born out of shallow ideas. One is frequently told that miners and sailors are a sort of social riff-raff and that evolution from the individual to the herd—the natural, expected-of-God procedure—is materially halted by them. Perhaps the clear, hard Colorado air paradoxically acts as a sort of solvent, for after

1860 it wasn't long before Colorado's mining men had welded their community together, developed a patriotism and a rigidity of moral code which stacks up with the rigid codes of more effete communities. And while the reader of the foregoing may feel that it is merely a record of an intolerable lawlessness, it must be noted that hand in hand with violation there stalked a most vigilant retribution.

Colorado was thought to be a land of promise from 1859 to 1893. Men would risk their lives to reach it. A. D. Richardson, a Boston newspaper man travelling to Denver with Horace Greeley in 1859, said: "It is a most forlorn and desolate looking metropolis." To-day it is a sprightly and well-ordered town of the bungalow era. Millions of gallons of water have been diverted from the snow runnels of Mount Evans and Mount Rosalie and grass has been coaxed to grow and trees rear their impersonal heads along the residence thoroughfares. A great civic centre of grass and limestone and marble has been bought and paid for out of a special improvement tax. It is pointed to with pride.

Urbanity has not been acquired without a stark, untiring effort, however. The heirs of those desperate men who came across the Kansas plains in 1859 pushing their push-carts, drying up of thirst, hiding their fever-soaked bodies from the roving Indians who flayed and scalped them whenever it seemed expedient, were not to be denied.

Men, huddling together with their memories and

their habits, will cling tenaciously to their inherited visions. The visions of pioneers are
single-track visions: to store enough water, fight
off enough savages, acquire title to enough natural wealth to insure comfortable old age and return to the softer life again. A. D. Richardson
relates having met a Missourian who, having lost
himself in the desolation of the "Smoky Hill" trail
across Kansas, lived for some days off the brains
of his brother. The latter, being the less hardy,
had succumbed to the unadulterated sunlight and
an unalleviated thirst. His skull was presented
as exhibit A by the survivor as proof of his determination to reach the Eldorado. Other instances
of like severity have been recorded, in particular
of one immigrant from Illinois who lost two
brothers along the same grisly trail and disposed
of them in a similar manner. The disposition of
a community made up of integers such as these is
likely to be somewhat relentless and unbending.

In 1864 Colorado decided to smash the Indian
menace. The Arapahoes and the Utes were the
aboriginal inhabitants of central Colorado, though
they held no recorded titles to their lands. The
Arapahoes held the plains and the Utes the mountain fastnesses. While these two tribes spent a
lot of natural strength in their tribal bickerings
they occasionally united to disturb the white man.
In 1864 they became extremely restless. They
blocked all the routes to and from the Missouri
valley so that a trip across in that year was thought
to be suicidal. The Civil War had stirred up cer-

F STREET, DENVER, IN 1865

tain notions in the aboriginal head that white
supremacy was on the toboggan. So the ranchers
in remote quarters began to suffer, began to lose
their scalps.

One night it was rumored in Denver that the
Indians were coming to wipe out the town. There
was tremendous excitement. Fires were lighted.
Women and children and some of the less hardy
males were crowded together into fireproof buildings. Outposts were stationed and sleep was
abandoned. But the night passed without un-
toward incident. Shortly after this episode the
Governor of the territory made a public proclamation in which he urged "all citizens of Colorado,
whether organized or individually, to go in pursuit
of the hostiles and to kill and destroy them wherever found and to capture and hold to their
private use and benefit all the property they could
take."

Colorado had a National Guard at the time under a Colonel John M. Chivington. The Colonel
had been a Methodist minister in Iowa or Ne-
braska before becoming a pioneer. His civic
responsibility had been high for a long time. The
proclamation of the governor made an impression on his stern nature. Like William the Silent
in the Bois de Boulogne, he received its import
without resorting to comment. Being titular and
actual head of Colorado's military forces he em-
barked to a council with some Indian chieftains,
among whom were Black Kettle of the Cheyennes
and Bull Bear and Left Hand of the Arapahoes.

The conference, like most disarmament confer-
ences, resulted in nothing more than some picturesque bits of oratory. The Indians were not
in the least servile; hardly were they courteous.
They held a lot of trumps up their sleeves. The
parley broke up in some confusion without an en-
tente cordiale coming to flower. Colorado's governor went to Washington on business and the
Military Commander of the Department, a General Curtis, delivered himself of the opinion that
the governor had had no authority and no right
to conclude a separate peace with the Indians
anyway.

Thereupon Chivington set out for the south
quietly on his own responsibility. He took his
regiment with him. In November he came upon
Left Hand and Black Kettle in camp about forty
miles south-east of Fort Lyon. Without parley
he set upon the Indians, having first seen that
their camp was well surrounded. A very effective
slaughter was accomplished. Of the nine hundred
Indians encamped, nearly every one was slain, including Left Hand himself who came forward
holding up his hands palms outward, signifying
that he knew when he had had enough. Chivington had ordered his men to take no prisoners.
They obeyed his orders.

Five years in Colorado, exposed to its natural
dangers, had taught the Colorado guardsmen the
best aboriginal practice. Among the victims of
their thoroughness were nearly all the Arapahoe
women and children. The white soldiers scalped

their victims and their work was said to be above
the reproach of the best aboriginal critics.

The victorious guardsmen returned to Denver
and were received by a committee from the
Chamber of Commerce and commended on the
thoroughness of their work. The city gave itself
up to a general rejoicing; business men meeting
each other on the street would shake hands and
comment on the fortunate riddance. Somewhat
to the surprise of the city, the event, later known
as the "Sand Creek Massacre," was labelled as a
deplorable incident by foreign chambers of commerce who, because of their remote point of view,
had not the proper sense of values and expedi-
encies.

"Sand Creek" is an evidence of the growing
homogeneity of Denver. And homogeneity being
the first necessity in any social gathering reveals
itself in a young city as an outstanding virtue.
For four years the body politic had labored to
preserve itself from forces of disruption within.
Then had come the need to preserve itself from
forces of disruption without. On the whole it
was a crystallizing process. Then in 1893 to meet
a great emergency, Governor Davis H. Waite
proposed to his legislature that if the Government
of the United States was shortsighted enough to
dispense with the coinage of silver dollars, thus
striking by judicial fiat at Colorado's foremost industry—the mining of silver—he, the legislature
and the State of Colorado should engage in the
coinage of silver dollars on their own account.

He proposed shipping the bullion to Mexico and having the money coined there to avoid certain awkward social formalities.

This manly recognition of the first law of nature was not endorsed by the representatives and Colorado slumped into the worst panic she has ever known. The governor's uncompromising gesture toward the great social menace of bankruptcy is not lessened in glamorous significance by the timidity of the agents of his people.

Denver is sixty-seven years of age. It covers an area as large as the town-site of the Borough of Manhattan. It has endorsed a slogan, "Five Hundred Thousand by 1930." From the number of street signs embellished with this slogan, she is going to do it or bust. Certain of her detractors say that she will never do it. For, they say, she has not the robust civic virtue she once had. Justice, having fattened on irrigated fields, her cheeks like red pippins from the bright sun and lusty winds, is becoming obese. She is a stay-at-home listening to radio programs. The robust Denver of the early sixties has become softened by an overpolite usage, they say. The stringy and hard bitten civic body has been taking on flesh and losing its sunburn. It has ceased to eliminate its natural body poisons in the natural civic way. There is a feeling that the sixty-seven year old town has overfed herself so obscenely that she no longer has the character to put her system in order or even to call in a doctor. These are harsh words.

It has been suggested in the foregoing chronicle

that Denver's early life was vigorous if nothing
else. Her rule of thumb was a simple one, made
up of articles six and eight of the code Mosaic.
But this simple code was enforced with what even
Denver's most rigorous detractors must admit
was a direct and prompt assumption of responsibility.

After 1860 the city may have begun to lose some
of its civic interest in the upkeep of virtue, turning naturally to other concerns. Women•came to
Denver. There is a biologic proof of that. And
hangings began to diminish in number. There is
visible proof of that in the records. How the citizens of Denver behaved privately in these years
is not recorded. That Denver did not differ materially in her private life from other cities is not
to be proved nor is there any desire to prove it.
There are many wild oats in every public granary.
Very little sex stuff appears in Denver's early
news sheets. But they were not printing that sort
of thing in news sheets anywhere in those days.

Then in 1892 and 1893 and thereabouts, one
notes in a careful perusal of the records that an
idea seems to have been bruited about to dispense
with certain practitioners—professional people—
certain filles de joie—to drive them out of and
away from certain regions around about Larimer
and Market Streets—away from Denver altogether.

But the merchants got together and without
ostentation effectively bashed the idea. What
could the dizzy theorists have been thinking of?

The world is always crowded and shouldered into uncomfortable corners by rattle-brained enthusiasts who have never paid any of the practical costs of "building up" a business or a city. "The Denver of the early sixties was a fine, upstanding town," these gentlemen assured their consciences. "Let there therefore be no picayunish interference with the private life of our 'who's who,' the gents who put us on the map." So for seven or eight years the town grew into adolescence. And while she suffered some financial misfortune in that time and grew a bit meagre about the girth as a result of the disastrous governmental fiat against silver, still she breathed in the free air of her great open spaces, was bluff and hearty of speech, ate with her knife and kept her self respect.

But along about the year 1900 a change seemed to come over the town. The joy of living began to slip behind some sort of shadow. The bluff and hearty transgressors of the social code no longer took zest in the moral maladversions that they used to take. There began to be heard an occasional "shush" when the maladversions of the foregoing generations were touched on conversationally. The head of the house may found a fortune but it does not automatically give him a permit to come into the parlor in his sock feet and suspenders, to spit into the gas grate or to rest his feet on the mantel. Once the level of the upper crust is achieved the mode of the upper crust must be observed.

In 1900 the pioneers of the sixties were ap-

proaching their three score years and ten. They
were likewise approaching a position of social
eminence comparable to the eminence of that
frost-bitten crew that landed on Plymouth Rock
in 1620. All their barbers, cooks, and sutlers began to acquire eminence. That some of them may
have eaten their companions in times of great
gastronomical pressure was not to be mentioned,
or if so, with the proper deprecation. Of course
the ends justified the means. And if there had
been any informalities in any matters of wedlock
—why, what was a man to expect in a mining
town? In short, while Denver was becoming socially conscious, while she was getting her first
taste of suavity, she showed a fine broad spirit of
understanding and forbearance. The attitude of
the merchants toward the ladies of Larimer Street
illustrates the point.

But along about 1900 certain private matters
concerning certain first families began to be noised
about. Along with the gossip and conversation
came some attendant snickering. It all seemed to
come from the same source. It was the sound a
pair of peeping toms make to each other between
gasps as they peer into a strange bed-room. At
first this behavior received the disregard that it
deserved. But it was repeated.

Time and again it was repeated. Down the
list of "who's who" went these naughty peeping
boys. No one with a financial rating escaped. Old
motheaten yarns of old motheaten adulteries began to go the rounds again. Now it is one thing

to hold up to light the sexual misbehavior of a
young and sprightly pair. And it is another thing
to lug out of camphor the old dead passions and
indulgences of a couple whose frangible bones will
no longer stand up under mundane stresses and
whose eyes have lost their lustre, and to trot them
up and down a runway for public speculation.
The latter somehow savors of passing around second hand cough-drops.

But the practice was not confined to baiting the
senile. Wild oats became a drug on the market.
If a young blade felt the urge of a spring fret,
it was up to him to take it to far distant pastures
or else be prepared to pay liberally for his indulgence in cash or exposure.

For it is not to be inferred that this new institute for the preservation and encouragement of
virtue owed its inception to any altruistic motive
however misguided. The gentlemen who controlled its destinies were merchants in the com-
pletest sense—not evangelists. They had come to
Denver frankly for the mazuma.

They had looked over the field and decided to
build up a market for silence. No one had been
peddling that commodity in the town up to that
time. No one had recognized the great opportunity. It was virgin country for that sort of
thing. Up to that time Denver had behaved
frankly and unashamedly as a child behaves
toward all adult taboos. In 1900 Denver was
reaching her adolescence. She began to have a
sort of adolescent shame of showing to strangers

her nude civic body. By 1900 many of the aesthetic values of the General Grant era had
trickled into Denver; the legs of its womankind
were not included in its symbolical picture of her.
In 1900 the new virtue merchants recognized with
discernment that the time was at its ripest for
their venture. So they went to work.

Silence being a negative quality owes its importance solely to its contrast with its antipodes.
One cannot measure the quality of a silence save
by a comparison with the racket which it displaces.
Its quantity of course is measured by the length
of its duration.

The price of silence, like the price of other commodities is to be determined by its quality and its
quantity and it likewise depends on the laws of
supply and demand. Hence to make silence valuable, the first step obviously is to make it a rare
thing. That is the first thing these itinerant merchant princes proceeded to do. In the early days
water had been the rarest, the dearest, the most
unique natural blessing in the town. In a few
months it was displaced at the head of the list of
community rarities. Man—Colorado man—forgot the sound of his great open spaces. Nature
lost her voice in the babel. The immigrant peddler princes knew their stuff.

Then customers began coming in. "What will
be the price of three years of silence concerning
my aunt Majolica?"—"I want to run for district
judge and I would like a six months' respite for
my character. How many franchises will it cost

me?"—"My bank is having a little rough sledding right now—last summer so hard on the stock, you know. What's the tax for keeping mum until we can get over the hill? Can I buy an exemption outright or do you folks want it on a royalty basis?"

To the superficial observer Denver is a fine, moral town. A clean town. The robust splendor of the early sixties apparently has not been dimmed. In the cartoons of her daily sheets the typical Denverite is always pictured as a somewhat dour gent in a broad brimmed hat with fat, capable hands and a banker's mustache, a trace of a paunch draped with a fourteen carat chain and a Masonic emblem. He usually stands in a manly if informal posture, taking a farmer or a laborer into his pleasant confidence. He is usually pictured as telling these latter that so long as they behave they may inherit God's footstool with him—that this Colorado of his'n is undoubtedly God's footstool, and that the climate like which there is nothing comparable was probably made possible by his farsighted and well chosen friendliness with the Almighty. Colorado *is* a place where men are men and it is a privilege to live. For there are no slums in Denver. There are no sinks of iniquity. There is no mud in the gutters, due perhaps to the fact that the dust there has never felt the degenerating touch of rain. Denver *is* a clean town.

But after a visitor to its well swept environs has begun to get the lay of the land, he begins to hear a few thin-voiced complaints, whispers in querulous key.

The self-same stereotype who rests his paunch on the gate post and disclaims so gustily about the weather is for the most part a fiction of the cartoonist. He is on dress parade for the Tourist Bureau. See him in the home and you will find him a bit bare as to hair, a bit run down at the heel, a bit runny at the nose, nervous and jumpy, furtive and blustery.

You will observe that he keeps a weather eye on his family closet. Never for one moment, while you are watching, will he get out of sight of the door of it. He may have in his pocket the receipt for ten years' silence, covering all members of his immediate family, his own past behavior, the reputations of all his progenitors. But he never can tell how soon an eldest son may see fit to fly off on a hideous tangent or a daughter run away with a soda jerker, making it necessary for him to rush immediately forth and draw up a new protective contract covering all these new idiosyncrasies. It's a rotten life for a man who knows his duty when he sees it.

It will be claimed that despite the imperfections of the system, virtue is its own reward. Perhaps it is. If so, then these peddler princes of privacy will doubtless be interred as to bones and gristle in some future American Canterbury, there to be revered as they deserve. But as is customary with most dogmatic saints their popularity is not marked. The bluff and ready Coloradoan who

makes such a fine show of crossing their palms
with silver so as to make the procedure simulate
the best business practice, in secrecy would like
nothing better than to have some of those sacred
bones to feed into some pleasant coffee mill.   In
the privacy of his club, in the comfortable corner
of his overstuffed divan, under the cover of the
harsh voice of his new "loud speaker" he may admit to himself, may even admit to some trusted
Damon or Pythias that "things ain't what they
used to be" and that "some day all this monkey
business'll have to stop."

Not so very long ago a certain Denver citizen,
owner of a large semi-public utility, was closeted
with a number of his peers.   The walls were her-
metically sealed.   Great doors shut out the Colorado sunshine.   This gentleman stood and delivered the customary platitudes.   And then he
began to yield to emotion.   But first he caught a
surreptitious look behind him.   Then he lowered
his voice.   "I'm a native Coloradoan," he whispered.   "I'm a Westerner.   And by God I'll not
stand for this sort of thing much longer."   He
paused and gulped dramatically.   "Some day I
may want to leave the state.   And if I do—and
if anything is—if there's any conversation about
it—or me—or mine—by God somebody's going to
be hurt."   He did not seem at all happy at the
prospect.

It is rather an odd contrast to the behavior of,
say, W. H. Middaugh, who trailed young Gordon
across to Coffey County, Kansas, thirty-two hun-

dred miles, with a rope and a six-shooter and a natural buckram along his spine.

A few months ago the Denver Chamber of Commerce issued one of its usual spawn of slogans. Due notice of it appeared in the birth and death columns of the Denver papers but no one saw fit to comment editorially, for the birth of a slogan of a Chamber of Commerce is now thought to be reasonably commonplace.

But the foreign press picked one out of the scramble and held it up for ridicule. Poor little thing, it was so weak and helpless it did not know what the laughter was all about. And its parents were covered with a natural confusion, not feeling too sure about it somehow.

This particular little slogan said:

"DO IT."

And then, following this positive adjuration, it appeared to lose some confidence, lapsing into a weaker, negative parlance. The words then ran:

"I will *speak* no evil.

"I will *hear* no evil

"Of Colorado and Denver.

"I will always

"*uphold* my State

"and City.

"Denver Chamber of Commerce."

The foreign press characterized it as mere Chamber of Commerce piffle. But actually it is more than that. It is the faint and plaintive protest of a community that has been threatened to death. Printed on red and white window cards

it appeared in thousands of Denver windows, on
the posts and fences of Denver. Of a certainty
there were some nailed to the physical properties
of the Bandit Virtue Trust itself.

There is a law on the statute books which for-
bids the buying and selling of silence. But the
law is helpless before an organized morality. So
it sits in its chair of state and mows and trembles
and gives off an occasional shrivelled cachinna-
tion. For the collectors of the Virtue Trust's
levy are not without a certain Rabelaisian humor
in the performance of their self-appointed tasks.

The Denver Chamber of Commerce is frightened lest the Virtue Trust may seek to peddle its
wares to the city. They are afraid lest the pure
white symbol of the city's honor may be sub-
jected to some adverse remarks. They shrink from
the display of her nude civic body. And lest they
be ordered by the Trust to "kick-in" with the
usual lagniappe in kind, they are voicing this
plaintive little protest. Denver's past, present
and future are not to be impugned. They are
attempting to build up a moral code forbidding
such a thing. And the Virtue Trust is laughing
up its sleeve. It knows what it can do.

As for the silence concerning Denver's past, is it
really worth anything—that silence? The old
Denver possessed at least one homely virtue that
seems lacking in the Denver of to-day. She had
adequate bowels for battle. She had the stuff to
keep her house in a sort of gusty order. And she
laundered her own 'scutcheon.

The Denver of to-day seems to be desirous of nothing so much as to keep her reputation clean. She seems willing to dust on a little rice powder over the dirt. She has no heart to come to grips with the Virtue Trust and she has the character to make a deal with them, a perennial contract for silence—civic silence—which the Virtue Trust merchandizes also. But fearing that the price which she may have to pay may savor of distortion she is predicating her civic need with the aforementioned slogan. Her civic wise-men are of the same stripe as the Punic merchants of Hamilcar's day. Fatuously they imagine that by the weight of their accumulated august presences they may bring the price of silence down. In their hearts they know better. All of Denver's élite know better.

The truth of the matter is: the Denver of to-day lacks guts. Suavity and slogans have bleached her to a poor anaemic yellow. Nice town, yes, but——

Just who is the Virtue Trust?

Write and ask any member of the Denver Chamber of Commerce.

SAN FRANCISCO:

A Retrospect of Bohemia
By
Idwal Jones

SAN FRANCISCO

ONE of those Stygian tule fogs had swirled through the Latin Quarter and got into our throats. My friend, a tenor of resounding fame, was apprehensive for his vocal cords, therefore we entered a bar in Columbus avenue and asked for strong drink. The barkeep looked as stone-hearted as Tagliagola, the Calabrian bandit. Prohibition informers had faces even more innocent than those of ours reflected in the mirror. And he had been raided twice. It was a critical moment.

"Ah, *un bel di!*" warbled the tenor. Tagliagola melted. His Bourbon was good. Then entered a personage. He was crowned with a huge *cappello,* and his cloak, smeared with clay and paints, was fastened at the neck with a silver chain like a bulldog's.

"Signori, an artist," explained the barkeep. "Mister Giovanni Muschio!"

Noblesse oblige, so we offered him a glass. Later, Muschio demanded that we be served with a dinner sufficiently worthy of us. So down cellar we went, a black cave alive with squealing rats. A light revealed a table covered with oilcloth and set about with decrepit chairs. Tagliagola banged pots on the stove and yelled infernally, and some quite charming persons came down: an Italian editor, a scene-painter, a fiddler and a singer among them.

A miraculous banquet was evolved: *gnocchi, vitello con salsa,* chicory salad and *zabaglione.* To drink there was Asti spumante, Tipo Chianti with wicker bellies, demijohns of sparkling Zinfandel. The talk was stimulating, an intellectual tornado. We made speeches that were vociferously applauded. Muschio eulogized our pleasant traits. Tagliagola arose, vowed that his life had not been lived in vain, then collapsed, through excess of emotion. It was that Asti. . . .

At 5 a. m. we encountered the dawn. Who paid for that fabulous dinner I never knew. It was not Muschio. We conducted him down Third street, among the Hellenic coffee-shops, while he looked up at the signs. Beneath one: "Beds. Two Bits a Night," he halted. Borrowing a quarter, he wished us a *buona notte* and disappeared into the flop-house of Big Gus the Greek. The tenor, being a man of fine instincts, wept, and swore he would live in San Francisco forever. However, he sobered up, and left that very morning.

After that, Muschio, in company with a Jugo-Slav painter, came often to my garret in California street to argue. A militant anti-clerical, he spoke with pride, nevertheless, of some years' time he had served on a Jesuit organ in Milan, writing editorials. His Russian was even better than his Italian, so much had he travelled. He

made living painting imitations of Zuloaga and
Gauguin—an incredible mixture. Heaven only
knows where they are. Probably in museums.
Some of his Gauguins were better than the originals.

Desperately hard up though he was, he enter-
tained in the most lordly fashion. The last affair
he staged in the chambers of a woman painter now
dead. He assessed all of us a dollar. He pur-
chased miles of spaghetti, boiled it in a baby's
washtub borrowed from the Jap housecleaner
downstairs, and made a bucketful of sauce. These
feats he performed over a gas-burner, up in his
attic. The comestibles were hauled off in a cab,
and he stopped en route at an undertaker's parlor
to buy a pair of white cotton gloves.

The dinner was a splendorous success. The
stuff was edible. That man could have made a
ragout of a tough hippogriff. Muschio donned
the gloves and dished out the paste by handfuls.
We were short of tumblers. As luck would have
it, George Wharton James kept here his famous
collection of Pompeian tear-jars, and out of these
lachrymatories we sipped the blushful Hippocrene.

At "dress-up" feasts he always came two hours
late; and small wonder, for he kept his velours hat
at Bigin's, his cane at La Campana, his best
trousers back of the wine kegs at Buon Gusto, a
pair of pointed shoes at the Tour Eiffel, under
the bar, and his collars—he had forgotten where.

Even the best-certified Bohemians marvelled at
Muschio, the while they prophesied a dire fate.

The worst did come to pass. He visited Los
Angeles—some elderly lady had become infatu-
ated with him—and he tarried. Now this *gai
sabreur* has been painting scenery for Tom Mix.
The amount of money he makes must be prodi-
gious, and in frock-coat he rides about in a limou-
sine driven by a high-priced Japanese with a face
like a bronze.

He was the last of the guerilla artists, and his
defection caused no surprise. For Bohemia had
long been on the wane.

Muschio recalls the vanished triumvirate that
made the beer-halls of San Francisco the envy
of Munich: Tofanelli, a braggart of the first
water; Benvenuti, the eagle-faced and violent old
man whose forebears for generations had been the
official painters at the Vatican; and Cristodoro, a
fat and morose genius whose taste in gnomes,
kobolds, Gothic landscapes, and cavern scenes
with a mediæval flavor of rapine and bloodshed
made beer-drinking at the Louvre, the Olympia,
the Zinkand, the Pabst and the Tait an emotional
experience.

The merry and turbulent days were dying out.
More thoroughly than Baron Haussmann had
changed Paris, the fire of 1906 had transformed
San Francisco. The *genus loci* had been inciner-
ated. The old haunts were destroyed. The energy
of the people was absorbed in the task of recon-
struction, and there was a hiatus in the artistic
life until the building of the exposition.

When the lath and stucco city began to rise on the Marina, the painters and sculptors, who had fled elsewhere, drifted back, and with them hundreds of European craftsmen. That task completed, plastic artists did gingerbread for the architects. The brushmen got jobs with the poster companies. A thousand lots within the city limits were screened about with hoardings that concealed craters filled with weeds and fused brick. So billboard painting became the principal art of the town.

The *affiche* has progressed in San Francisco beyond anything done this side of the Atlantic. Collars, ginger-ale, butter-substitutes, Coca-Cola, hats, automobiles, chocolates, bifocal glasses, vacuum cleaners—these are emblazoned on the noblest billboards west of the Mississippi. At night they are dressed up with electric sparklers. A majestic Navajo—a Maynard Dixon Indian—stands on an illimitable desert and contemplates a salmon-pink sunset. The moral is to buy somebody's tires. But what of it? This is a commercial age, and to paint such is remunerative work.

The aesthetic nature of the present generation has been nurtured on these billboards, just as in England the prose style of the most esteemed writers has been formed on Eno's Fruit Salt advertisements. The billboards are vanishing before the triumphal progress of the concrete-mixer, and must soon take refuge in the far hinterland.

Some ten artists are painting pictures to hang on walls. There are still homes left to put them in. But the majority of citizens are genuinely urban and dwell downtown. Even millionaires live in midget apartments, for the immigration laws have made the problem of domestic help more acute than ever. The wall-bed is a San Francisco invention, and when the contraption preempts too much of the wall space for anything to be stuck up larger than a photograph.

Where are the Bohemians of yesteryear? Gone into commerce, and prosperity has befallen them. They keep respectable ménages in "gum finish" apartments. And they are probably all at home. Call up any of a score, and no longer do you hear the significant, and sacramental phrase: "The line is temporarily disconnected."

The writers? Gone to New York, where all the publishing houses in the country are. They don't commit the folly of shooting at long distance when they can make a killing just a block away and save postage. The weekly periodicals that bred a superb crop of literati here in the previous three decades are non-existent. Folk used to lay in a supply of local weeklies to read over the week-end as religiously as they brougdt home the sabbatical gallon of steam beer.

Golf and the automobile have usurped Sundays. But what killed the weeklies was the distrust of periodicals that were not standardized, that were not precisely what people read in New York, Chicago, Boston and everywhere else. The urbane and erudite stylist, who seasoned his articles with the salt of *in situ* allusion, was damned as provincial. He hadn't a chance against the rotogravures of bathing beauties.

Prohibition, of course, wrecked the topography of Bohemia. Gone are all the haunts, from Marshall's of Bret Harte's day, where the romancer discussed sherry and baked venison marrow with the prototypes of Oakhurst and Jack Hamlin, to the last of the *botteghe* raided in the Latin Quarter, where the bright spirits foregathered to spend unlimited hours at trifling cost and cultivate the fine art of conversation.

Leveroni's, the gayest of cellars; Maggini's, renowned as the stamping ground of the wits of the "Suicide Club"; Lucchetti's, famous for its "breadball" barrage and fried halibut; Papa Coppa's, with "the jug behind the door," the rendezvous of the Irwins, Jimmy Hopper, Jack London, George Sterling, Martinez, with the bandeau over his Aztec locks, and the seigniorial Ambrose Bierce, dropping in after visits to the Morgue where he had gone to inspect the "floaters" in from the bay; Negro and O'Brien's; the early Fior d'Italia, otherwise the "Fire of Italy," where newspapermen were ranked one notch higher than the lesser angels—the litany is now like a strain on a Louis XIV harpsichord.

Reverent souls will point out their sites for you. They are soft-drink parlors, or they are placarded with those saddest words of tongue or pen: "This Corner to be Remodeled to Suit Tenant."

At times a Latin pities those whose souls were once warmed with the ichor of the true Falernian, and starts a cenacle. The hired snifters creep in. They gladhand the illuminati, bedevil mellow talk on paint and words, and after indefatigable efforts succeed in inducing the cook to give them a sip from the kitchen sherry bottle. Then a badge is flashed; everybody gets hauled off to the Bastille, and broad and genial tolerance is once more foully slain. And in a state where viticulture but a few years ago was glorified as the noblest of arts.

Civic indulgence perished before the onslaught of the Methodist forces in 1916. Their leader was an Iowa Savonarola, the Rev. Paul Smith, pastor of the Central Methodist Church. Their first objective was that roaring spectacle, the Barbary Coast. Roughly, it embraced Broadway and Pacific street, where the Thalia, the Wave, the Swede's and a score more dance halls gave entertainment to lusty youth from the mines, the lumber camps and the deep sea, and the adjacent alleys where twinkled the lights o' love. It was in a mean part of the town; less flagrant than the Paphian belt of New Orleans, and little more wicked, though more noisy, than the Cannabière of Marseilles.

The vice-fighting parson let loose his philippics. The police commissioner protested that the region was more orderly than any in Chicago or New York, but the row was on. The pastor threatened to print a roll of dishonor with the names of the plutocrats who owned property in the district. The city quaked with anticipation, but the idea

fizzed out like a damp farthing candle, for only
an obscure real estate agent got shown up—much
to his annoyance. Then the pastor organized the
Law Enforcement and Protective League, with
himself as president and a Y. M. C. A. secretary
as promotion manager. All the professional wow-
sers rallied under the banner and fought with the
exaltation of mullahs. The *filles de joie* were
aghast, then consumed with indignation. They
appeared in a body at the Central Methodist
Church, and made their complaints likewise at the
City Hall.

But the game was up, and the alleys were puri-
fied. The dance-halls were abolished, the French
restaurants chastened, and the beer-hall devotees
disciplined to the meekness of Quakers at a meet-
ing-house. The vice-fighting parson paused not.
He determined to carry his reform all over the
United States. The first step was to employ the
movies, and to film the great fight as an object lesson. So "The Finger of Justice" was made. The
church scene was filmed with the Reverend Smith
in his own pulpit, supported by a vested choir of
thirty-six, with the pipe organ going at full blast,
and the congregation in the throes of hysteria.
Gilded sin was depicted in the cabaret scene, which
cost $5,000. Little Jane O'Roark, attired in shim-
mering scales, writhed as the vamp; Crane Wilbur,
star of "The Perils of Pauline," had the hero's rôle,
and the Rev. William L. Stidger, an able young
ecclesiastic, now in Henry Ford's entourage, es-
sayed the part of the cop.

Two hundred Methodist persons attended the first showing, and shattered the canons of their church by sanctioning the Sunday exhibition of the film. Inspired by his meteoric rise to the front pages, the Rev. Paul Smith resigned from the ministry to become head of the International Church Film Corporation, and left for New York. There, much to the chagrin of the League, the license commissioner of the State, one Gilchrist, barred the film as subversive of public morals!

The Barbary Coast, boarded up, is now the haunt of stray cats and mechanics contemplating the opening of small tire-repair shops. Otherwise it is as deserted as the North Pole, except at eight o'clock of evenings, when the Salvation Army, ever faithful to the spot, bangs the tambourine and exhorts the empty air, exorcising the ghosts of dead sins. On the boundaries, below stairs, are dismal and empty Little Bethels. At times a Jack Tar strolls through, striking matches to hunt for once familiar numbers, and then hies himself to a Wild West movie or to blaze away fifty cents at a shooting gallery. The Los Angelization of San Francisco is almost complete. The latest innovations are orange-juice stands and buffoons in costume ballyhooing in front of the movie palaces. The passion for uniformity rages. Until recently the town had a complexion peculiarly its own. But not now.

The annals of San Francisco are vast and extravagant. In the seventy-five years of its existence there was more fulgurous life than in three cycles of Cathay. In a twinkling a trading post had become a Gargantuan camp which the turbulent youth of fifty nations transformed within a decade into a city of the first rank. The town had become old before it ceased to be young. It had a Bohemia from the very beginning.

The first Bohemian was Jacques Raphael, the witty chef-de-cuisine of the old Tehama House. He had been *cordon bleu* at the Rocher de Cancale, Paris—the rendezvous of Balzac's Rastignac. Alexander Dumas rhapsodized over his baked partridges. When the roi-citoyen Louis Philippe went to pot, Murger's Bohème died the death, and Mons. Jacques quit France, in a great hurry. The next year gold was discovered in California, and in a tent pegged down on a San Francisco sanddune the once illustrious chef, in top boots and sombrero, was ladling out slumgullion à la Mazarin to the Argonauts.

La carrière ouverte aux talents! That was Mons. Jacques' brave device. He advanced to omelettes à la Morny, made from seagulls' eggs. His sauce to disguise the fishy flavor was a culinary triumph. His business grew, and he put up a huge corrugated-iron shed. Spanish aristocrats, Mississippi steamboat gamblers, sailors, the frail sisterhood, gunmen, Sydney "coves," miners insane through sudden wealth—these poured riches in Mons. Jacques' lap.

He formed a cenacle that included the wits of the camp: two nephews of Victor Hugo, the fiery Lola Montez, just banished from her Aspasian couch in Bavaria—surely the man had talk and charm enough about him. San Francisco, a city of sand-hills, tents, sheds, Peggotty houses made of ships sunk in the teeth of rifle-fire by schemers preempting the waterfront lots; a city harried by the cutthroat "hounds" and policed by the no less dreadful Vigilantes—it was not Paris. But Mons. Jacques enjoyed himself hugely.

That summer the first artistic event was held— a concert. The solid citizenry attended en masse, with the Governor and his staff; the barbarians tried to "crash the gate," but were repulsed by the gendarmes. The front row was reserved for the ladies, and four hetairæ availed themselves of the privilege—the entire house standing until they were seated. The affair was a terrific success. The cheering was maniacal, corybantic. Canes, hats, chairs were hurled into the air. It would have turned the head of Taglioni or Fanny Elssler. Mons. Jacques declared, "It was a Romantic demonstration that eclipsed that over 'Ernani.'"

What was the feast? Merely a spectral tenor, a Pierre Gringoire who had been dining through his nose, warbling "Take Back the Heart that Thou Gavest" at a tinkly piano in the schoolhouse. That tenor was Steve Massett, later renowned for having eaten a whole cooked goose at a New York salon.

Above the tower on the Butte Montmartre in Paris clanked a semaphore. Atop Telegraph Hill in San Francisco, an eminence destined to become the Montmartre, nay, the Parnassus, of

the western world, likewise clanked a semaphore.
The analogy pleased Mons. Jacques. He died, a
satisfied exile, and was promptly forgotten. The
candle of *la vie bohémienne* had been lighted by
one of apostolic succession.

So far the boundaries of Bohemia had not been
defined. Attics were let out at fabulous sums.
Social unorthodoxy prevailed. What is Bohemia
but a minority revolt against provincial narrow-
ness? The town was gay, sprawling, uproarious
and peopled by men tolerant of mind and by nature nomadic and lively.

By the middle fifties Bohemia, such as it was,
was the milieu of dandies, viveurs and gentlemen
of fortune. The high-rollers consorted on Merchant street, massively built up with brick edifices
reinforced by iron doors and shutters, and hardly
wider than an alley. The gourmands were to be
found at the Ivy Green Saloon where Bass's Ale
was to be procured. Bolton and Barron, the
quicksilver kings, had here their offices and ban-
quet-room; their chef was paid twice the salary
of the President of the United States. He cooked
the fifteen-pound turkey, washed down with twenty bottles of sherry, that the corpulent banker
Eugene Duprey consumed at one sitting to the
awe of the assemblage. He won a bet of $500
thereby. Without, like a crowd by the Quirinal
awaiting the result of a Papal election, were
throngs of *tribudores* come up from the mines,
arrayed in velvet jackets bedecked with silver
buttons, their faces stained red with cinnabar ore.

As the crapulent hero strode forth, they cheered him as rapturously as the Florentine populace acclaimed Giotto or Cimabue. The poet O'Connell celebrated that feast in measures right worthy of Ossian.

What passed for the aristocracy kept house in South Park. It was gotten up like Kew Gardens, and here cattle barons, shipping masters, bankers and diplomats gave routs and dinners to three hundred people at a time. Young bucks drove thither to ogle the damsels promenading from Mlle. Zeitska's Female Academy. Bewigged footmen stood guard at the portals. Trades-persons went around to the back areaways.

Within ten years this citadel of the bourgeoisie had become shabby genteel, so fast were the changes in the social fabric. Mons. Louis Bacon, drawing master and sculptor, tendered himself daily in this park, with snuff-box and clouded cane. So far as I can learn, he was the first artist. He was "bang-up society." Also he did funerary art, and his stone urns and weeping-willows still evoke the megrims in the abandoned graveyards.

By happy chance, he ran into a Maecenas, one Ah Sing, an adept in Chinese rituals who kept a private joss-house. Ah Sing was a master-hand at funerals. Flute and drum players, banners, immense dragons a block long, drays hauling a thousand roast pigs to lay upon the tomb—customers got a run for their money. Ah Sing had his little vanities. He was wont to bestow largesse upon all artists who made a good portrait of him. Mons.

SAN FRANCISCO IN THE LATE FIFTIES

Bacon made a cartload of statues of his illustrious patron, and was able to retire shortly after. Grief among the artists was unutterable when Ah Sing returned to China in 1870, his departure hastened by the police.

The sixties were a prosperous decade for the artists, who found it the Land of Cockaigne. The town was large and as substantial as Boston. The very exuberance of the people, their prosperity and undisciplined taste gave birth to a rococo, an efflorescence of ornaments that was astounding. Exteriors were tricked out with pagodas, bell-towers, porte-cochères, garbels and verandas, laden with serpentine carvings and colored windows. Homes were crammed with ormolu, bronze Arabs, cozy-corners of spears and draperies, sculptured fruit and lacquered cherubim. The lawns bristled with cast-iron fauna. Domesticity and the pseudo-arts interpenetrated.

Bohemia, peopled by souls in revolt, became acutely self-conscious and localized. Most of it was to be found atop a fortress of a bank on Clay street—penury above the money-bags. The spirit of Señor Arriola, a painter of oil portraits, pervaded the establishment. He had been drowned off Acapulco on a return home to visit a fickle innamorata. From Red Dog and Whiskey Gulch came red-shirted miners to climb the stairs and get their pictures made to send back East. Nobody would do but Arriola!

These customers were obliged by Pascal

Loomis, the dog painter, or else by Charles Brooks, the salmon virtuoso, or Jules Tavernier, who did landscapes. A delightful coterie, all of whose names were illuminated on Arriola's door.

That door was unique among all doors in the world. It was nearly a foot thick, made of solid oak, and placed at the head of the staircase, like a barricade. That effectively shut out ruffians. Arriola had carved and painted his coat-of-arms upon it. This procedure was followed by the elders. In fact, to have one's name thereon was an honor surpassed only by achieving the Prix-de-Rome.

A most amiable little man was Brooks, the doyen of the group. The accuracy with which this Meissonier of salmon depicted scales was the despair of both artists and icthyologists. His method was simple enough, he stencilled them on, using a square of Brussels lace. He burned with simple fervor before his masterpieces. No painter had a larger heart. He had taken a lease on the entire floor, and sublet studios only to impecunious artists. He lent them cooking utensils, got tick for them at the butcher's, and saw that the vintners furnished them with the necessary claret.

Between Brooks' establishment and the Julien and Gerome ateliers in Paris flitted men of undeniable gifts. And here lived the incomparable Harrington, who painted Madonnas and *quattrocentista* saints. The other day a prizefighter took us to Jim Griffin's, the referee, whose saloon is about the only landmark left of the old Barbary Coast. Above the bar was an excellent little painting of "Andromeda Chained to the Rocks," with flesh tints and a palpable modelling all too rare. It was a Harrington. We lament that we know of no other example of this joyous Dionysian save that gem in the Andromeda Saloon.

A burly, roaring Celt, with a bulbous nose and plug hat, very much like a hackney-driver, Harrington was the cock of the walk until the advent of the Gariboldi.

This paragon of Bohemia arose in the middle seventies. He entered a café on Montgomery Street, and called in such stentorian voice for a waiter, that words died on the lips of the patrons —journalists, models, artists, actors and the like. He threw back his dolman to reveal the blood-red lining. He demanded a salad. Some wit, to mock him, likewise ordered a salad. Then fish, a dish of paste, etc. The wit echoed each item.

"Wine in a quart glass!" sang out Gariboldi.

"Wine in a quart glass!" shouted the wit.

By this time the whole café was in turmoil. Gariboldi twisted the head of his cane and pulled out a glittering rapier, felt the point, and with a muttered imprecation, thundered:

"A sword, *cameriere!* And bring it sharp!"

The death-like silence was broken by cries of delight and a fusillade of handclapping. Gariboldi sprang full-panoplied into renown. The town was full of originals, but none more picturesque than Guglielmo Gariboldi, whose aspect and unique talents dumbfounded even Bohemia. The times were made for him. He had marked the city for his own, and with his sword split it open like an oyster.

This was the era of the colossal. The treasure-box of the Comstock Lode had been broken open. The Ophir, the Yellow Jacket, the Chollar-Potosí poured into the town a deluge of riches. Great as was the display of the mining magnates, it was outdone by the railroad kings. The last spike of the Southern Pacific had been driven in, and the newly-crowned kings spent their wealth in San Francisco.

Mark Hopkins, the Southern Pacific financier, was building his castle on Nob Hill. The granite wall, with bastions and portcullis, about the lot, cost a million dollars, and the house, a masterpiece of the Pullman school, cost two million more. It was admittedly a fright.

Gariboldi arrayed himself like a Grand Duke, with epaulettes, spent his last dollar on the hire of an imposing equipage, drove up and demanded the job of furnishing that house. He got it. The commission was close to $100,000. The Napoleonic Hopkins quailed before those personal grandeurs and that challenging eye.

Once a month Gariboldi, with his acolytes, jogged down with a buckboard to the railroad offices for payment. Sweating clerks loaded the rig with two pine boxes, like coffins, filled with $10,000 in gold coins. The horses could barely crawl up Pine street to the cottage, and an escort of Bohemians aided the ascent with shouts and pulls on a rope.

The counting of the specie lasted until midnight. These nights were celebrated with a saturnalia of roast ducks, bouillabaise and champagne. We have met aged men who shed tears at the recollection of these Neronic feasts.

"Il Magnifico" has left no trace behind him. The theaters he decorated in his flamboyant style; the Hopkins chateau, with its frieze of wooden angels—naught has survived the fire.

It is to his elder contemporary, Pietro Mezzara, a Sicilian stonecutter, that San Francisco owes what vestiges remain of its traditional Bohemia. He deserves more than a footnote, for he was the first sculptor to make a statue of Abraham Lincoln. Not that good Pietro was a rabid Republican, or anything like that. He deplored the laxity of the Jeff Davis protagonists in not raising a fund and getting something equally handsome. But the fact is indisputable that this was the first Lincoln, and so Mezzara is secure of his place in the hagiology of the West.

The statue weathered forty years in front of a school on Market street. Lincoln was depicted as a fiery Balmaceda, thrusting a document at the Powers of Darkness. Even Harriet Hosmer—disciple of Canova and Gibson though she was—confessed to a shudder as she passed by. It was a piece of wartime bravura, and its loss in the disaster of 1906, is to be measured solely in terms of sentiment.

A creature of extraordinary zeal, Mezzara helped found the art school. It was perched over the California Market, a popular *charcuterie* and fish-shop down town. This was a happy propinquity. Whenever a pupil or master was seized with the pangs of hunger and lacked change, all he had to do was to knock off a canvas and trade it with the clerks downstairs for a steak or a plate of tripe.

The school throve mightily, like an indigenous plant. The Cytherean, though often foggy, air of San Francisco was propitious to the aesthetic spirit. The mass of the students was Anglo-Saxon. The leaven was Italo-Gallic. The *élan* of such leaders as Mezzara infused the academy with a heady self-consciousness that manifested itself in fêtes of volcanic gaiety—masquerades with Afghan chiefs, Corsairs, houris, Amazons, the cahut, the can-can and the galop infernal. With what glee the tragedian Salvini describes these Paphian revels in his memoirs!

Decorous beyond reproach is social life at the academy these days. It has become an adjunct of the state university, and the elders regard it with patriarchal benevolence.

Some years ago a philanthropic dentist plastered the city with statues of himself, cast in a Connecticut iron foundry. They were of a horrific ugliness. A band of valiants headed by Gelett Burgess made a sortie under cover of darkness, lassoed the statues by the Ruskinian pot-hats and hauled them to the dust. The dentist clamored for capital punishment. The Board of Supervisors was apathetic. What could one say to artists?

Two months ago at the annual art exhibition, the Brahmins were aghast at a small nude hung on the wall. The lady, forsooth, had no shirt on. She savored of *La Vie Parisienne*. So down she went to the basement, though the Grand Jury had awarded her a prize.

Art in San Francisco is still praised, though regarded as a little bawdy. But not for worlds could we dispense with that vague entity known as Bohemia. The journals without some lickerish reference to artists, those high-priests of nudity, or to some lunatic raving in free verse about the moon would be as savorless as the breakfast egg without salt.

Pleasant, pleasant fellows those artists we used to meet in brighter days. Economic pressure had not ground the iron into their souls. In that rookery on Polk Street, the last redoubt of Bohemia, there were a dozen it was a high privilege to know. It has been torn down to make way for an ornate apartment house. Rent was high at ten dollars a month, but the landlord could always be stood off. Claret was fifteen cents a quart. They sustained their virtues, pride and ideals on the occasional sale of a sunset or "View of Mt. Tamalpais."

There is small room for them now in the busy world, and still less for their old haunts in the Latin

Quarter. Rents have shot up in that region designated by mastodonic electric lights as "The Heart
of Bohemia." Parnassus is heavily over-capital-
ized. The Café Momus is become a spaghetti
Versailles. At the door stands a giant Senegam-
bian in brass buttons and shako.

Where congenial souls once talked over the slen-
derest consummation—that corner is cataclysmic
with a jazz orchestra whanging and bellowing off
key while a chocolate-colored lady in green ballet
skirt gives an imitation of Sophie Tucker. Touch
not the *pasta*. Even the Italian waiters are
looking flabby and scrofulous through lack of the
antidote for excess of gluten—the tannin present
in the fermented juice of the grape. Their look
of hebetude is due to the speeches of the Rotarians
and the Civic Improvement Club members they
have had to wait on. It were enough to debilitate
the most rampagious *Camorrista!*

Telegraph Hill, groomed and fitted with a
palisade for the protection of tourists, is now a
park. Down the slope flutters the wash of some
surviving artist, and it flutters in the salt breeze
like defiant oriflambs. The bay-scape is by Tur-
ner, palpitant with haze and whorls of mist-
scarves blown in through the Golden Gate. Disposed in broken planes of grey and purple the
city lies on a dozen hills. The colors would delight Veronese.

Under the group of eucalypti whose fronds
clatter in the wind sits an artist with coat collar
buttoned up. He faces the heart of the city, look-

ing down Montgomery street, the purlieus of the old Bohemians. He adumbrates with gusto the towering shafts of the Telephone Building, the Standard Oil, the Dollar Line, the Pacific Gas and Electric—the enormous piles springing up in accordance with the new art of vertical design. These are the tongues of the city, the tongues of a great metropolis. They are calling him. He packs up his kit and whistles for a taxicab. He has to deliver a snappy talk on color in commerce before the Ad Club.

The mirthful, leisurely Bohemian days are gone with the provincial ways that conditioned them. *Vale, messieurs*—the play is ended. It was an infinitely amusing spectacle.

SAINT PAUL:

The Untamable Twin
By
Grace Flandrau

ST. PAUL

A S is well known, St. Paul, among western
cities, is not like other girls. She did not rise
from the blue shirt of the miner and the lumber
jack, the diamond studs of the faro king or the girl-
ish ladies of fifty odd who dazzled the frontier with
their mauve face powder, gold fillings and lemon
colored hair. On the contrary, she took off at a
different point altogether and although she has
made vast and solid progress in the columns of
Dun and Bradstreet, her career has been, in certain other respects, a descent.

An army post, a great fur company, an amaz-
ing mad Utopian in Scotland, Indian annuities,
and the Catholic Church, in the person of a young
French priest with a singularly fine and charming
face, are all concerned in the origins of the city.

In 1819 what is now Minnesota—then a part of
an immense indeterminate region known as
Michigan Territory—was a country physically
co-eval with the Garden of Eden. Aside from half
a dozen quite insignificant exceptions, it remained precisely as it had blossomed forth after
the last glacier oozed its slow way southward a
few eons ago—if that, indeed, is what the glacier
did do. The insignificant exceptions were a thin
scattering of fur-trading posts set down here and

there on lake and stream in the great stillness of the wilderness.

These posts had been established by those gallant, high living, hard drinking, aristocratic privateers of commerce, the Nor'Westers of Canada and a rival company known as the Mackinaw, and were operated by them with great profit and success. But the earnest attention of a rather formidable gentleman in New York City, Mr. John Jacob Astor, had been focussed for some time on the exodus over the border of American furs, taken from American Indians and producing what should have been American dividends. By 1816 he had brought about the passage of an act forbidding any but American citizens to trade with the Indians within the territorial limits.

The North West Company moved across the border and the American Fur Company, owned by Mr. Astor, took over the posts. It retained the French-Canadian *voyageurs* and *engagés* and much of the tradition of the Canadian company. Young Americans were put in charge of the posts and in some cases Frenchmen who belonged to the old company hastily took out Americanization papers and remained in the business.

The government now sent out expeditions to explain matters to the Indians. It must be made clear to them that they had an entirely new Great Father, must respect a new flag, no longer wear medals bearing the effigy of King George III, and, above all, never trade with the British across the line. But the Indians showed a marked preference for their previous Great Father, for the whiskey, trade goods, flags, medals and appurtenances in general of their old friends the North Westers and, encouraged by the latter, traveled across the border whenever possible with their furs.

To combat British influence with the Indians and protect American trade and American traders, it was decided to construct the forts along the new frontier planned for some years earlier. Fort Snelling was accordingly built during 1819-22 at the confluence of the Mississippi and Minnesota Rivers—a strategic point between the territories of two great warring tribes, the Chippewa and the Sioux. Within the precincts of the military reservation an Indian agent was established and across the Minnesota River (then called the St. Peters) at a place known as Mendota, the American Fur Company established its Northwestern headquarters.

In 1834 a young man of twenty-three, Henry H. Sibley, a clerk and later partner in the company, arrived to take charge of the establishment. His appearance on the scene marks, in my mind, the real beginning of St. Paul.

We must, however, before we proceed to the portentous moment of its birth, briefly glance at a most curious and seemingly irrelevant personage, the Scotch Earl of Selkirk. This interesting gentleman was of all Uplifters one of the most determined and bemused. The victims of his passion for service were certain evicted Scotch and Irish peasants and, later, the downtrodden of other

States, lured doubtless from their native lands by inspirational advertisements setting forth the advantages of the new Utopia.

This is not the place to tell the singular story of this undertaking. Suffice it to say that shiploads of protegés of the good earl were discharged on the semi-arctic shores of Hudson's Bay and obliged thence to make their painful way seven hundred miles southward by canoe, on foot, or on snowshoes to the vast domain he had bought for them north and west of Minnesota in Canada. They settled on the Red River of the North near the mouth of the Assiniboine and there for some years they variously froze, starved to death or were butchered by the *bois brûlés*—a crew of savage half-breeds set upon them by the North West Company, which objected to having its trapping grounds spoiled by settlers.

We however are only interested in a band of Swiss watchmakers who, driven out, it is said by floods, grasshoppers, and rats, escaped from Selkirk's Utopia and made their way southward to Fort Snelling. Here some of them remained, under the quite erroneous belief that they would be welcome on the reservation. They were not. They were twice compelled to move from their houses and small plantations under a misapprehension as to the extent of the military reserve. At last they got safely off it and established themselves on what has since become the center of St. Paul's business district.

There was in the vicinity of Fort Snelling and

especially at Mendota, a considerable sprinkling
of French and half-breed *voyageurs* who had settled there with their families—enough good Catholics to warrant the maintenance of a priest among
them. When the Selkirk pilgrims started a new
community across the Mississippi River from
Mendota the good father decided they too must
have a church. So in the year 1841 he built a
log chapel among them and called it St. Paul's.

I am aware of an irreverent rumor that the
City of St. Paul really derives from a slough several miles south known as Pig's Eye. An occasional writer still states that St. Paul was originally known as Pig's Eye. This is not the case.
Father Galtier records that the small community
of Pig's Eye was indicated to him as a possible
location for his chapel, but that he chose the Swiss
settlement, as it offered the best steamboat landing in the whole region—a fact of immense significance in the history of St. Paul.

Besides the docile Swiss agriculturalists, the
only non-military residents of the region were the
before mentioned hangers-on about Fort Snelling
and the trading post at Mendota and, strung
safely along the east bank of the river, which was
neither military reserve nor Indian land, the
whiskey traders, who nefariously inebriated both
soldiers and savages. These various elements
gradually congregated at St. Paul's during the
earliest days, and French was almost universally
spoken there. But the men who were to occupy
positions of prominence and power and to put their

stamp on the community did not rise from this stratum. They were superimposed upon it. They were for the most part Mr. Astor's, or later Mr. Chouteau's, young men, imported from the Eastern States to take charge of their posts in Minnesota:—Pratte Chouteau & Co. of St. Louis, bought out the Western branch of Astor's business in 1834.

Now the fur business, which was about as ethical as buccaneering in the days of the Virgin queen, was nevertheless the aristocrat of commerce. From the time when Prince Rupert, cousin of that most fashionable Stuart king, Charles II, became president or general manager of the Hudson's Bay Company, it has possessed tradition, manner, a certain *chic*. This the Nor' Westers inherited from the Hudson's Bay, and the American Fur Company took it from both. When the good old Nor' Westers set out from Montreal to meet at the half way house on Lake Superior the wintering partners from the far west, their birch bark canoes carried silver plate and champagne and French cooks into the wilderness. They took their valets to dress them for dinner, polish their silver buckles, and disengage them from the débris under the banquet table when the still forest dawn stole into the lofty dining hall at Fort William. But it was not all champagne and silver plate. There was an aristocracy of character that must not be overlooked.

The factor in charge of a remote fur post was carefully chosen and was a kind of king. His power was absolute. His job was difficult, dangerous, and delicate. His *voyageurs* and *engagés* were ignorant, wildly superstitious, and unruly. He must establish a lasting ascendancy over them. He had to satisfy, overawe, and exploit savages who outnumbered his men hundreds or thousands to one, and inspire in them both fear and liking. The Indians were as capricious, intuitive, unreasonable, and sharply intelligent as children and as sensitive to personal quality. They recognized and intensely responded to dignity, courage, and good manners. Those men, it will be found on examining the history of a period now gone forever, who had the widest influence with the American savages, when the latter were still powerful and to be feared, were not only, as Ouida would put it, Men but Gentlemen,—if gentlemen in the Elizabethan rather than the Methodist Episcopal sense.

The men who dominated early St. Paul and whose power continued long after pioneer days, were with some notable exceptions, fur traders. Not the free, so called whiskey traders, but the representatives of responsible firms—chiefly the American Fur Company. And while St. Paul was a ruffian infant of "birch roofed cabins and whiskey shops" these men were still scattered about the territory in charge of their various posts.

It is too bad that there should have been no contemporaneous chronicler with a salty tongue and an eye for reality, to have made adequate portraits of those young adventurers. All Western Americans are familiar with the thick biographical subscription books full of beards and bombast which have visualized for us the daring, roystering, serious, law-making, law-breaking, law-enforcing youngsters of the frontier. We see them as middle-aged rabbis in frock coats, with all the playfulness of a Baptist undertaker burying a Rockefeller. I think by the time pioneers get old and have paid many fifty dollars to have their autographed steel engraved portraits in many such books, and each and every one has an Hon. in front of his name, they think of themselves that way.

But there really was a time when they were young and wore, not beards—oh, I believe they did, even in their teens—but beaded moccasins and coon-skin caps and bright sashes, and danced Chippewa mazourkas at Long Kate's and at all night balls in the cabin of Bottineau, the half breed.

There was young Sibley at Mendota: a crack shot, expert canoe man, so good a boxer that in the whole territory only "Bully" Wells could stand up against him; head of the American Fur Company's wide spread business in that region, and, when scarcely out of the twenties, justice of the peace of a county as big as several European states; a power among the formidable Sioux, so liked, trusted, and feared by them that no government negotiations could be carried on without him.

There was Henry M. Rice, like Sibley a young man of excellent family and striking personal dignity, trading now among the Winnebago, now among the Chippewa, obtaining over them by the charm, courtesy, and tact of his address an ascendancy which surpassed if anything Sibley's power with the Sioux. Both men were to win national responsibilities and distinctions later on.

Oakes, a young New Englander, and Dr. Charles Wulf Borup, a cultivated Dane, represented the Fur Company at Yellow Lake and later became, in St. Paul, the first bankers of the territory.

At Pembina on the Red River of the North, just south of the Canadian line, Norman W. Kittson traded with the Chippewa and the French Crees and shipped furs, buffalo tongues, and pemmican to Mendota in the famous Red River wooden carts. He himself frequently made the long journey on snow shoes or dog sledge, not seeing a human habitation during the whole five hundred miles. Later he was to enter into partnership with James J. Hill. Their steamboats were to navigate this river and Kittson was to participate to some extent in Hill's great railroad enterprise which opened the valley to immigration. Kittson was a step grandson (whatever that may be) of Alexander Henry, early explorer, trader, and partner of the North West Company, whose diary is the most revealing and fascinating piece in all the original literature of the fur trade.

Martin McLeod, stationed at Lac qui Parle, was a Scotch Canadian described by a contemporary as, "a man of commanding presence, cul-

tured intellect—eloquent, dignified and charming." With the annual supplies sent to him
through Sibley, went important historical and
scientific works and French classics in the original.
It was to McLeod that later much excellent educational legislation was due.

I have alas seen no notice that these gentlemen
were teetotalers or that they failed to fight and
swear and, frequently, during the hot political
fights of the fifties, to fall out with each other and
fling about unpleasant epithets and accusations
which, however, always failed to stick. And as to
women it may be said that one or two of them married their squaws but mostly they didn't. In fact, I
think it is likely they were many things (the
possessors of good manners included) which some
of our Latter Day reformers would have
condemned wholesale. Yet their forcefulness,
breadth of view, public spiritedness, loyalty and—
whatever the accepted ethics of politics or the fur
trade—their personal integrity have seldom since
been surpassed. In the late forties Minnesota,
which had been successively a part of Michigan,
Iowa, and Wisconsin Territories, decided to become a territory herself. Sibley was sent to
Washington to bring it about and in 1849 the object was achieved. Minnesota Territory was created with St. Paul as capital city.

The fates were kind to the infant community.
The administration was inspired to send out as
territorial governor a man actually fitted for the
job. The happy appointee was a former Con-

gressman from Pennsylvania, Alexander Ramsey by name. The territory was at this time enormous, including besides Minnesota much of the Dakotas and extending westward to the Missouri River and so remote that the Ramseys' neighbors wondered whether they could reach it by sailing round the Horn or crossing the Isthmus of Panama! It had a large savage population and presented difficult problems as regarded Indian affairs, Indian trade, and the pressure of immigration already impatient to cross the Mississippi and overflow the Indian lands beyond.

The territorial governor was thirty-four, young it seems, but older than most of the men who were making the history of the state. The frontier, however, could be a beneficent and powerful teacher. Let this memoir from the pen of a man who was later to achieve many distinctions speak for these youthful adventurers, of whom he was one:

"If a young man of ability migrates to a country over which no government has yet extended, he finds himself confronted with the solution of large issues. Fundamental and philosophic problems force themselves upon him; he becomes an original thinker himself and finds a virgin field on which to test the experimental creations of his genius."

Ramsey was abundantly a man of ability. He promptly and efficiently organized the territory, convened the first legislative assembly and delivered four remarkable messages, practical and prophetic, shining with common sense and with real wisdom. The legislative session opened, we are told, "with prayer" and as the governor and many of the influential members became St. Paul's foremost citizens, it is pertinent to glance at its activities.

Besides routine administrative measures, much of the legislation was, to quote a contemporary, "of a moral and educational nature." It provided generously for free schools, founded a historical society, righteously established stringent Sunday laws, prohibited sale or gift of liquor to the Indians and licensed the general sale; while at its second meeting in 1851 it decided upon and made ample provision for the creation of a State University, and also this remarkable body of frontiersmen revised the code of laws left over from the previous régime and did it well.

Sibley was sent to Washington as territorial delegate; H. M. Rice, Borup, Oakes and other prominent traders came to St. Paul to live; James Goodhue, the notable editor of the first newspaper, the Pioneer, began his brief but brilliant career in St. Paul. He was aggressively a Puritan; he stood violently for law, order and virtue—so violently indeed that within three years he had died as the result of a shooting and stabbing affair.

He had, as was the journalistic manner of the day, roundly insulted a political opponent. The brother of the latter stabbed Goodhue three times in the stomach while Goodhue was engaged in shooting at him. The populace joined in the fray and a brief but lively scene of stone throwing and clubbing took place. Both of the principals died subsequently as a result of the encounter.

But occurrences such as this were rare; St. Paul was, for a frontier city, decidedly orderly. It must be remembered that precisely at this time California gold called like a siren from the Pacific coast. But the long transcontinental journey was full of danger and the reward at the end as problematic as the fall of dice. It was the adventurous, the high spirited, and the desperate who streamed across the deserts and over the mountain passes to the Pacific—those who despised danger or disdained work or were expert in relieving the lucky of their easy money. A very different class proceeded safely up the Mississippi in comfortable steamboats to the city at the head of navigation. The heroic days of the fur trade were about over; the pine forests, waiting to create a bright new galaxy of millionaires, had not, although exploited to some extent, as yet attracted widespread attention; the richness of the iron deposits was of course not known. Climate, natural beauty, the privilege of hard work in the fields, and the commercial possibilities of a growing river port were the solider and more prosaic lure of Minnesota and attracted a corresponding class of men and women.

As to commerce, the Indian trade must not be overlooked. I have said the fur trade was declining. But the Indians were receiving large cash annuities for lands sold to the government, and St. Paul and neighboring posts were the disbursement headquarters. To the traders who flocked to the payments with their beads and kettles, blankets, whiskey and bright calicoes, specie was even more welcome than muskrat skins. The gold passed through the hands of the Indians as through a sieve, into the coffers of the trader-merchants, and thus the infant St. Paul was nourished to prosperity.

The Sioux lands immediately west of the Mississippi were acquired by the government. The city grew rapidly. A constant stream of immigrants flowed through the small port. Professional men of considerable distinction—lawyers and journalists in particular—attracted by the beauty of site and healthfulness of climate, perhaps too by the reputed "gentility" of the place, arrived and became part of the pioneer body.

The prominent pioneers married and for their wives went back to the places and generally superior social class from which they themselves derived. Ladies in flounces and sacques and long lace mitts and tiny perched-up hats, holding bottles of smelling salts in their hands, stepped daintily off the gangplanks into the mud of the levees and brought to their frontier houses, smelling of new pine lumber and frequently of Sioux and Chippewa callers in smoky blankets, the manner of life to which they had been accustomed.

In 1854 the Chicago and Rock Island railroad was finished to Rock Island, Illinois. In truly modern style the management organized an excur-

sion. A large group of prominent Eastern people
were invited to make the trip over the new road
and on up the river in steamboats to St. Paul.
Twelve hundred important and highly respectable
persons, including "many of the divinity," are said
to have accepted and to have returned to the East
spreading lyrical reports of the beauties of the
wide river, the wooded bluffs, flowering prairies,
sweet untarnished air and gracious stillness of this
empty Eden known as Minnesota. A particularly
modern note which I cannot refrain from quot-
ing is the sermon preached by one of the enthusiastic divines: title, "Railroads in the Higher and
Religious Aspects." "My hearers! Some of
you have tickets that will lead you to Hell. The
car of death is hastening on. We urge you to
change that ticket. Christ is always in his office——"

All in all the publicity which followed the excursion helped to increase the enormous incoming
flood of people the following year. St. Paul went
into a boom state. Real estate soared, interest
rates soared—to 5% a month; everything and
everybody soared; fine raiment and high stepping
horses appeared; gamblers, speculators, crooks of
all kinds—a most un-St. Paul-like type of people
began to arrive. Then the panic of '57 struck the
little city like a cyclone. Banks broke; money
practically disappeared; the dubious high financiers fled away to more propitious fields, and St.
Paul gradually settled down into the stride that
has been hers ever since.

Once more the fur trade came to the rescue.
About this time the Hudson's Bay Company abandoned its long established canoe route via streams,
rivers, the Great Lakes, and the St. Lawrence to
the Atlantic. It began to ship its furs in bond
by Red River ox cart to St. Paul and thence by
steamboat and railway to Eastern ports. The
long trains now swelled to five hundred carts and
driven by the picturesque *bois brûlés* screamed on
ungreased wooden axles to the St. Paul levees.
When the carts returned down the Red River valley to Canada they were filled partly with goods
sent in bond from England, but also with supplies
bought from the merchants of St. Paul.

Let us now glance at the foundations of St.
Paul's social life as they were being laid in these
important fifties, and as they have endured pretty
well into the present century, almost to the time
of that nemesis of all foundations, the late war.
That they had been thoroughly shaken and were
on the verge of collapse some time before hereditary St. Paul would dream of admitting it, is not
surprising. Hereditary St. Paul—and the core
and kernel of the city is still hereditary—does not
admit things and never has admitted them. To
err is human, to admit it is cynical. And St. Paul
abhors cynicism. But to go back——

I have before me some letters. They were written during the fifties by three New England girls
who came out at different times to keep house for
their brothers in the Indian trade. Somehow,
these letters give one rather a heartache—they are

so young, feminine, superior, mid-Victorian, and real. And now all the writers, so sure of their good breeding and immortal youth, are dead. I knew one when she was an old woman—touchingly like the girl of frontier gentility.

A few extracts may epitomize the beginnings of fashionable St. Paul.

"This has been such a week of dissapation; Monday we were all invited to a pleasant little mob at the governor's; it was a truly enjoyable party and very select. Tuesday a brilliant party at Fort Snelling. The general handed me to table. I wore my flounced muslin and pink sacque with three rows of lace about the neck and two about the sleeves. Wednesday Miss B—— and the Colonel came in a buggy and we went a strawberrying; Thursday night a tableau party at the F——'s; Saturday there was a surprise at the S——'s; the governor was my beau for the evening and the first thing he did, I had hardly got there, when he came up and wanted me to promenade. So I took his arm."

The polite "dissapation" seems to have been pretty continuous. "We were asked to Mr. and Mrs. W——'s at the Winsor House. There were just enough ladies to get up a cotillion." Again: "A fine dance at Mazourka Hall. Not too many of the newcomers, so quite select. The ladies dressed finely in white satin skirts and lace illusion over dresses." Again: "The general sent his aid to invite us to a review of the Light Cavalry at the Fort, and to attend a party in his quarters afterwards. The first officers of the country are here to attend a court martial and there are three young ladies from Virginia visiting. It was very select."

The pest of lectures too was in full swing as the decade advanced. Mr. Y—— talks on "Europe: Their Manners and Customs"; Mr. L—— on "The Next Generation"; an Armenian missionary on "Syria"—"Church crowded and they put seats in the aisles. He was very smart." Again: "Bayard Taylor lectured on Moscow last evening. It wasn't much."

Calling, it seems, was a veritable monomania. "I have thirty or forty calls to make this week; We do not call at the Y——'s—she is not quite a lady. I called on Mr. R——'s bride. Felt I must. 'Tis said her father was a mechanic in Hartford and that she has been a governess. Too bad to let such a rumor get about. The general is bringing that Mr. Sumner of Boston to call. I have on my delaine and black silk apron. When not busy I put my hands in the pockets. I have got my rosettes on my wrists. Thursday the Judge and Baron Jaw-Breaker" (a Swiss baron) "called and we went to their saloon for ice creams. Sabbath morning attended service at Christ's Episcopal, though we usually go to Mr. Neil's" (St. Paul's beginnings were strongly Presbyterian). "Mr. R—— and Mr. S—— attended us home. In the afternoon three gentlemen left cards but we were not receiving. Monday the boys got back from payments. Brought Hole-in-the-day and two other

Indians to call. Then Peter brought an Indian
Agent from below and wife to stop. I was glad
when they left, they were such *plain* people. New
Year's Day we had sixty calls, not so many as last
year. I wore my black with red sacque, flowing
undersleeves, and mitts."

As to New Year's Day I will quote from the
memoir of a prominent jurist: "My first New
Year's Day in St. Paul was in 1854; it was my
entrée to St. Paul society. Four of us, all frisky
young fellows, started with a good team and made
one hundred and fifty calls by midnight. Whether
we drank at every fountain that gushed for us on
that day I will leave to the imagination, after
saying that only the vaguest and most delightful
impressions of the event linger in my memory."
Indeed the terrific gentility of this upper circle was
in no way impaired by the notable prevalence of
excellent wines, chiefly champagne, at all their
gatherings—picnics, dances, Indian treaty and
political meetings, dinners, and teas. And the
champagne seems always to have been set off with
oysters. Now as oysters in Minnesota even in these
days of rapid transportation are something of an
adventure, their presence in that epoch of summer
steamboats and winter stages (occasional and most
uncertain stages) does not cease to puzzle.

We will take leave of our New England sisters
with one more quotation:

"Tom and a member of Congress have been
waiting two days for François P—— to guide them
to the Indian country. But he is after an actress.

Bah—think of them waiting two days for him to gallant a dancing girl. And Sunny Marsh too, gone as far as Galena they say, with that Sally St. Claire!"

For alas, a far racier company existed outside the select circle we have visited. It was made up of free traders, whiskey sellers, French mixed bloods and drifters of all kinds. Among the latter, a contemporary writes, were "many gentlemen of refinement" who "being too fond of their cups came here to overcome the habit. The worst place," he adds with conviction, "they could have chosen."

One of the earliest meeting places of these convivial spirits was the bar, sitting room, "and everything else" of Jackson's house—whence at late hours they often repaired in a body to one of the informal all night dances perpetually going on in the houses of the French half breeds. It also appears that most of the gentlemen who so punctiliously left cards, attended pleasant little mobs, handed the flounced ladies to table or walked home with them after one of Mr. Neil's excellent sermons, were the handiest of all with the demijohn at Jackson's and similar hardy resorts.

St. Paul, however, was not without its growing body of "plain people" who frowned alike on the champagne and oysters of the upper crust and the trade whiskey and half breed balls of the lower. Of these the immortal spokesman is the author of an edifying opus called "Floral Home." The lady came out as school teacher and also opened the first Sabbath School, though not without misgivings that the "Romish priests" and "emissaries of Papacy" might interfere with the attendance.

In a chapter classically headed "Rum's Doings," she writes:

"The *bottle* was the unfailing attendant on *every* occasion, and stood confessed the life of *every company.*" She attended an excursion to the falls of St. Anthony in company with the "first citizens." When the refreshment was produced she was impelled to observe severely that that was the first time in her life she had been in a company where it was used. "Then," replied a gentleman whose elegance of manner she had previouslv noted, "you are entitled to the first drink."

Follow truly horrifying and doubtless quite true instances of Rum's black doings in the community; murders, suicides, delirium tremens, and the frequent accident of tumbling into the snow on winter nights and freezing to death. Then, in the midst of the "moral darkness" about her, she hears of the beginning of a temperance society. "Victory, Victory, Victory," she cries, only to deplore later in mixed and disillusioned metaphor that, although the organization had "laid the ax at the root of the tree—the monster, with its thousand heads, lives on."

She is much shocked by the nakedness of the infant and semi-nakedness of the adult savages, and the frequency with which they preferred their own superstitions and the "way which goeth down to death" to the "claims of the Gospel." Nevertheless, in revealing a proposal of marriage made to her by a young chief she does not fail to advise us of his proud, graceful dignity of bearing, his magnificence of ornament and apparel, his eagle eyes and rich sonority of voice—and piquantly adds that, upon being refused, he tried (unsuccessfully) to borrow a dollar.

The writer did not suffer from a lack of congenial company. The region seems to have been pretty well dotted with missions, and churches of all denominations multiplied rapidly in St. Paul—where they were enthusiastically supported.

Important events meantime had been taking place; Minnesota Territory had become a state with Sibley as governor, and an attempt been made to change the capital from St. Paul to St. Peter. This undesirable measure received a majority of votes and would have been carried had not St. Paul's leading citizens resorted to a simple device. The committeeman who had the important bill in his keeping was induced to hide in a hotel bedroom where he remained, quite drunk, until the time limit for the act to become law had expired. He has since developed in local tradition to a semi-saintly figure and is called the savior of St. Paul.

Rice, as United States senator, fought for land grant railroads; important but, at the time, abortive legislation was passed and the sixties came in without a mile of railroad completed in Minnesota.

The Civil War, long threatened, now broke out, and the following year a smaller but more immediate catastrophe took St. Paul curiously by surprise. The community had maintained the usual smug attitude toward the Indian, characteristic of pioneers since the days of the Puritans, who first "fell upon their knees and then upon the Aborigines." The St. Paul citizenry did not precisely fall upon the aborigines but it fell upon their titles and annuities. Subconsciously it denied their right to exist; it never dreamed of looking upon them as human beings, but simply as nuisances—irrelevant objects who were very much in the way: "The Indians have the small pox. Never mind, it will do them good," writes a young trader.

So we see St. Paul in lace mitts, unimaginatively dancing cotillions and drinking tea on the extreme edge of a savage abyss—a region lately the property of a race still essentially belonging to the stone age: a race which, as realization dawned and it saw itself without land and most of the time without money and food, forgot the half understood treaties and burned with hatred and revenge.

Quite suddenly, a thousand of the immigrants who had been deposited on the levees of St. Paul, or had plodded through her unpaved streets in prairie wagons and settled in the "Suland," were butchered, thousands of others driven from their homes and their property destroyed.

Ramsey, once more governor, acted with his usual efficiency and promptness. While Flandrau, extemporaneously in command, turned the Indians back from New Ulm, the Civil War recruits collected at Fort Snelling were put under Sibley and sent in pursuit and the rebellion was ultimately put down.

With the termination of this affair, St. Paul's frontier period may be said to have closed.

For the next twenty years pioneer names and personalities dominated to a large extent the administrative, legal, banking and social life of St. Paul, although politically such powers as Doran and Kelly had arisen to control the Democratic party; and the brilliant Cushman K. Davis had appeared to become one of the stars of the Republican—of which Ramsey, territorial and state governor, United States senator and cabinet minister successively, remained the outstanding figure.

Other new and important forces were at the same time quietly developing. Long before the arrival of railroads, the head of navigation of the Mississippi was a natural transportation center. It was the objective point of wilderness travel by canoe, dog sledge, and wooden ox cart. The chief articles of early traffic—buffalo robes, fine furs, jerked meat, pemmican, tallow, Indian work— came up the Red River valley from Pembina to the trading post at Mendota and later to St. Paul. Here they met and were transferred to the steamboats ascending the river with supplies from St. Louis, Galena, and the gradually approaching railroad heads. After railroad building began in Minnesota, St. Paul by orderly economic sequence continued to be the chief transportation center of the Northwest; while the simultaneous growth of her key industry, the wholesale business,

ST. PAUL IN THE SEVENTIES

was equally a by-product of the location of the city
and a logical progression from the early Indian
and river trade. It is from this developing
merchant class, far more than from the gallant
frontiersmen, that the actual St. Paul derives.

During the seventies and eighties the place grew
from a straggling, unpaved village to a small city.
Its social life, following the lines laid down in the
fifties, continued select and complacent and church
going, but put on more elaborate metropolitan
luxuries and frills. It went on, with some exceptions, keeping its doors firmly closed to "plain
people" and was augmented by newcomers from
equally select circles of Eastern and Southern communities. The question "Who was she?" continued
severely to be asked.

Turreted, spired, porticoed, cupolaed "palatial
residences" began to be built along the sightly
avenue that commands the river; fine driving and
saddle horses appeared, flashing carriages, high
tandem carts, unicorns, and four-in-hands. I like
to think of the beautiful and dashing Mrs. ———.
It took two grooms, we are told, to hold the horses
she rode and when she dismounted she patted the
foaming nostrils of her steed with handkerchiefs of
solid real lace and then lightly tossed them in the
gutter.

Champagne and oysters continued to be pleasantly prevalent, venison, pheasants, wild geese,
quail, and prairie chickens still enhanced the loaded
dinner tables. Bank presidents loaned money on
the security of good friendship and the glamorous

memory of frontier adventure shared. Money as
such had not mattered seriously in frontier times;
gain was always overshadowed by adventure; new
beginnings were easy to make. The pioneer tradition was, for the most part, lavish, casual, and
elegant. Then along came the financial hurricane
of '93 and blew down all the cupolas that were
not very firmly hooked into a rock foundation—
and many of them were not.

From this time the character of St. Paul
changed. The nabobs of the fifties and earlier were
getting old and dying. They left no fortunes. The
influence and character of the merchants began
more and more to be felt. They were not adventurers, but preëminently business men. They
built slowly and firmly; they saved; they put the
seal of their solidity upon the city.

Slowly too the formidable personality of James
J. Hill, one of America's greatest commercial and
far more than merely commercial figures, had
emerged. As this is St. Paul's story and not Mr.
Hill's, we shall not dwell on his achievement. He
made St. Paul the headquarters of his powerful
railroad, with its rock-like financial foundation, its
vitality, its capacity for continuous growth. It
peopled the Red River valley, the northern reaches
of Dakota, Montana, Idaho, Washington, and Oregon. The road was Mr. Hill's personal creation.
He did everything but lay the rails and punch
the tickets. The government had no part in its
financing and, as many of Mr. Hill's stockholders
and associates were men of financial eminence in

England and on the Continent, as well as in New
York, St. Paul, through him, became a figure in
international commerce.

Its reactions toward Mr. Hill are interesting.
It has sentimentalized him as a poet, prophet, seer
and saint; cried him down as a man-eating tyrant,
the assassin of Dutch bondholders, poor but honest
trainmen and suffering superintendents; has given
him torchlight processions and accused him of
throttling St. Paul by turning it into a One Man
Town.

This dire and cryptic reproach has been especially advanced as the reason why Minneapolis,
a city situated some miles west of us, should have
somewhat exceeded us in population. The One
Man theory quite overshadowed other reasons for
the greater development of Minneapolis such as
the huge flour (and originally lumber) mills which
her water power created; the preposterous immen-
sity of the State University situated within her
borders; the singular civic enthusiasm of her leading citizens—to say nothing of my own private
theory that it was also brought about by her possession of a large population of shrewd, long
headed Scandinavians instead of our corresponding
immigrant class of soft speaking, darling, shiftless
Irish from Galway looking toward the Arran Isles.

The one way that Mr. Hill did contribute to
the growth of Minneapolis rather than St. Paul,
was by populating the Great Open Spaces to westward with agriculturists who, when they came back
to civilization to spend their hard earned dollars,

struck Minneapolis first and stayed there until their money was gone.

But it must not be supposed that St. Paul spends much time in deploring census reports or anything else. The whole point is missed if St. Paul is not shown as she is, or at least has been most of her life—notably satisfied—complacent I should say, if the word did not carry a slur.

And I would not have it carry a slur. Complacency is what we need. Americans and American cities suffer from a disguised inferiority complex. That is the reason for all this boosting, bragging, and community-spirit-izing the hard boiled business of making a living.

St. Paul, in spite of the advent of many important and powerful newcomers is still, at the core and kernel hereditary. The sons and grandsons of the sound merchant and banking class, still give their stamp to the community—Griggs, Gordons, Saunders, Finches, Deans, Noyes, Ordways, Skinners, Lindekes, and many others—the fortunes they have inherited were not made quickly or speculatively, a tradition of conservatism has been handed down with them. Also they are safe and considerable enough so that their owners do not feel the urge that makes boosters and go-getters. Undoubtedly, like almost everybody else, these men want more money than they have and try to get it, but like civilized people they do not gloat and sing hymns over the process and talk about "service not gain" and indulge in the many tedious hypocrisies which some people sum up in the word Rotariarism—

whether fairly or not I cannot say. I have no personal knowledge of Rotarians, or of their alleged first naming, back slapping noon orgies. Although they do boost, the first gentlemen of St. Paul keep it rather dark; although they join things they do it languidly. They are not 'joiners" at heart. Yes, they are still individualists in this age of lodges, slogans, and alleged community spirit.

When something really important to the city has to be done they occasionally (our civic spirit is notably not robust) do it. But they do it under the leadership of one of their own coterie, a man like Gordon for instance, grandson of Dr. Charles Wulf Borup, far more than through the commerce organizations, which they, like the citizens of other modern communities, nevertheless maintain.

There is the Association. A vague murmur will arise about its having "brought the Ford plant, the Armour packing plant, Montgomery Ward," and so forth. Personally I believe it more probable that these prizes were captured by the method outlined above. Wishing to be fair I wrote and asked the Association what it had done. I quote from its reply:

"Do you wish facts relative to the Saint Paul Association or the city of St. Paul? Your letter clearly asks for 'literature describing the aims and achievements in St. Paul of the Association.' "

I did not write again fearing that they would once more assault my dazed ears and eyes by observing, You have told us quite clearly what you want—What is it?

Socially St. Paul has conformed: that is to say, society in the sense of exclusiveness or even of a somewhat petty snobbishness, the sense that prevailed from the fifties well into the present century, even until the war, does not exist—the society that meant and exacted "background," good manners, the appearance of morality, and the concealment of knees, thighs, and other innocent anatomical phenomena. Individuals possessing the old standards, as they are called, exist in surprising numbers in St. Paul, even in large groups, but not as a united and controlling group, not as society. Has jazz come and to a certain extent conquered? Hereditary St. Paul, which, as we have stated, does not admit things, says no. Personally—but then I am not, in that sense, hereditary St. Paul.

Doubtless the core of the business life will succumb to the modern mores; perhaps it is already definitely beginning to do so. When it does there will be even more Ford plants, bigger and better slaughter houses and vaster census returns. With which hereditary St. Paul will (at heart) be rather bored. It is satisfied with its size, it loves its wooded boulevards curving about its sightly river, and what still remains of the quiet of its elm and oak shaded avenues. How many times have I heard it complain of recent developments?—

"If this goes on we'll get bigger and bigger, and then," they exclaim aghast, "we might as well be living in Minneapolis."

PORTLAND:

A Pilgrim's Progress
By
Dean Collins

PORTLAND

EIGHTY odd years ago, Portland, Oregon, landed on the map of the Pacific Northwest, possessed of a full developed New England conscience and fleeing from the wrath to come. It was sired by New England traders, out of the settlement of Methodist missionaries at Oregon City, twelve miles up the Willamette River. It came into existence a comparatively ordered community, planted on the soil of two civilizations that had preceded it. This made it needless for Portland—like so many other frontier towns—to build law and order all anew.

The peace and civilization of the Hudson's Bay Company had dwelt in the territory at the confluence of the Willamette and Columbia rivers, earlier in the century where Dr. John McLoughlin, the "White Eagle," ruled like an emperor. That order was not concerned with the taming of the wilderness, so long as the Redskin refrained from murdering British subjects and continued to bring in the furs with which the streams abounded.

Hudson's Bay civilization was succeeded by the Methodist missionary civilization at Oregon City. This was founded by one Jason Lee, now by way of becoming the prize canonized Protestant of the Northwest. As occasionally happens to saints

without regard to sectarianism, this Lee lost his
job soon after his conversion effort approached an
efficiency basis.

His mission diverted its attention from the sal-
vage of Indian souls, first to the spiritual needs of
the incoming trickle of white immigrants; then to
the grabbing of the fertile lands and water rights
of the Willamette Valley; and at length to the final
stripping of Dr. John McLoughlin.

McLoughlin had flown in the face of Hudson's
Bay policy when he saved the missionaries and
settlers from starvation and massacre by the Indians, had resigned his almost imperial position at
the head of the Northwestern territory of the company's widespread activities. He had cast his lot
with the people he had befriended, in the town of
Oregon City, which he had laid out years before
and to which he had welcomed the Americans.

The result of his choice was a cynical spoliation
at the hands of the missionary leaders and settlers.
It would have made Æschylus of Eleusis weep
tears of pure esthetic joy, could the tale have come
to his hands as material for majestic tragedy.

The heads of the mission settlement, having
already possessed themselves of commercial control and of the lands of the Indians and of the
deposed factor of Hudson's Bay, efficiently took
possession of the political government as well, and
Freedom began slowly broadening down from precedent to precedent. As a climax to all this, Portland the Metropolis, Portland the Victorian outpost in the Wild West, came to pass.

It was a synthetic town built on a site predestined for a great city. The immediate cause of its existence was a bar in the Williamette River that interfered with F. W. Pettygrove, late of Portland, Maine, in getting freight boats up to Oregon City, loaded with goods. So among the cedars on the river bank, where William Overton, another of The Founders, was splitting shingles for the Vancouver market, Pettygrove built his storehouse and advertised his wares for sale "at the Red House in Oregon City and at Portland 12 miles below." It was just as convenient as Oregon City had been, to the settlers from the Tualatin Valley.

After Pettygrove had the town site properly surveyed, a settlement clustered about his store under the trees and in less than two years a school was opened (1847, if dates are of any interest to the reader). In the year following, the First Methodist Church was established on Taylor street between Second and Third, facing North. Thus Portland hit her stride.

But almost under a different name. A. L. Lovejoy flipped a coin with Pettygrove, in a controversy as to whether the town should be named Portland after the latter's native city, or Boston, after Lovejoy's.

However, it could not have escaped the flavor of New England in its name, regardless of how the penny fell. That was in the blood which nourished brains that could think of names of no other flavor.

Soon the Portland stride lengthened and became more pronounced. Came sailing around the Horn the Rev. Horace Lyman, of Massachusetts, and gathered the strong Congregationalist group together and founded a church. The Rev. James Croke opened a church at Couch and Fourth streets, under the wing of the Catholic organization that had antedated the Methodist invasion of Oregon City and which was—and still is—active in Indian missionary work. The Baptists, alas, gathered themselves together and had a zealous congregation by 1854.

All of this progress went forward normally. One of the early Congregational ministers, the Rev. P. B. Chamberlain from Maine, set the community by the ears, with an attack upon secret societies in general and Masons in particular. ("There were no Masons in his congregation," says an Eyewitness who still survives, full of years and grace, "but some of their wives were.") In the controversy that followed, eighty members of the church "swarmed" and formed a group which they called Presbyterian, while the original congregation dropped to ten members. Later the insurgent group returned to the fold and a formal foundation of a Presbyterian church was not made until 1861 a few years later.

The minister whose sermons had precipitated the trouble was dismissed after failing to resign. A million square miles of wilderness might roar behind her back in glee unsanctified, but the infant Portland cherished the blessings of religious

controversy like a child precociously "called" to
the ministry.

Meanwhile, Jewish traders coming up from
Sacramento and San Francisco laid the foundations of the great department store systems that
control the retail life of Portland to-day. More
incidentally they founded Jewish religious groups
almost simultaneously with the Christian developments.

So Portland traded and prospered and grew,
while General Ulysses S. Grant and Phil Sheri-
dan and others who later made Civil War history,
then stationed at the Vancouver army post which
had succeeded the old Hudson Bay's most westerly seat, did their apprentice work by polishing
off Indians. Within a few hours' modern automobile ride from Portland, settler volunteers were
riding their ponies to death and eating them in
order to have strength to commandeer other
ponies to ride to death in the task of stamping
out the last resistance that the Indians opposed
to conversion by the white man. Eventually the
Indians were converted—into tragic reservation
figures, wasting rapidly away under the too sudden change from a nomadic life to the complexi-
ties of pants, squirrel whiskey and a conviction
of sin.

And with each crisis, Portland's moral stride
lengthened. From his headquarters in Oregon
City, 1847, George Abernathy, provisional governor and steward of the Methodist Mission, issued an encyclical calling attention to the use of

liquor on the part of some members of the flock and the Washingtonian temperance society was founded.

There came no dash of godless fire to singe out the mature Puritan flavor of the Oregon settlements, in the big transcontinental covered wagon immigrations between the late thirties and the middle fifties—for Fate sat at the forks of the Oregon trail and winnowed the oncoming swarms. California, just wrested from Mexico, offering the lure, first of adventure and then of gold, drew southwesterly from the Oregon trail, the young men, the unattached and those whose temperament did not fit in with the sober responsibilities of settling and tilling the soil.

The family men, the men with instincts for settlement and development rather than adventure and exploitation and those who earnestly felt the importance of filling up the land with enough American settlers to keep the Oregon country from coming under the British flag—these came on into Oregon and there blended readily with the Puritan civilization that had sailed round the Horn in advance and possessed itself of the cream of the land. Churches rose almost instantly with the planting of each new community and the stern New Englanders resumed the doctrinal controversies that their grandfathers had begun in Massachusetts. Those grim, eccentric, heroic figures, the pioneer "circuit riders" paddled the streams and rode the trails carrying their Bibles in their saddle-bags, bearing spiritual comfort to the outlying settlers, and diverting their harassed minds from the imminent fear of starvation and scalping parties, to the imminent dread of the wrath to come.

The circuit riders knew no fear and gave themselves no rest and Oregon prospered and stood firm in the faith. Except for minor lapses such as the liquor drinking against which Abernathy rallied the forces of morality at the outset, Sin bulked very small indeed.

So here we have Portland, morally mature and full of grace, shooting church spires toward the sky in half a dozen spots long before Vice in any of its more flamboyant forms had presumed to rear its head.

Just how little it figured—aside from certain gigantic and humanly almost impossible legends of venery that have sprung up around the figures of some of the earlier political and military heroes —is perhaps best illustrated by testimony from the same Eyewitness quoted earlier in this article.

"When did Vice actually make its appearance in Portland?"

The answer was given in perfect gravity:

"The first billiard table was brought up by boat from San Francisco and Jim Fruiht and Donald Stewart installed it in a saloon, in 1851."

Thus came Satan out of the Babylonish city of the South and entered—somewhat handicapped by belated arrival—in the titanic struggle for the Soul of Portland.

It is doubtful if Satan would have bothered to make the trip if there had been only the original settlers to consider—men of family busied with tearing a livelihood out of the soil and forests, and under the double inhibition of Puritan background and family responsibility to hold them from moral misadventure.

But some of the boys, who had grown up here after crossing the plains, went down in the Forty-nine gold rush and into the gaudy sophistication of San Francisco. They picked up some of the sophistication, even when they found no gold, and brought back home with them a taste for the world, the flesh and the devil.

Their wickedness, however, did not cause much head-shaking among the elders until early in the sixties. Then the gold rush swung North into Eastern Oregon and into the Coeur d'Alene district in Idaho and the Yankee traders in Portland found themselves entertaining a type of customer quite different from the harassed, careful and frugal settlers.

Their establishments became the headquarters for outfitting the stream of gold seekers pouring into Eastern Oregon and Idaho, for Portland in those ante-railroad days was the one point of contact with the Eastern cities that lay on the Pacific Coast nearest the district of the latest mining developments. Shipping increased around the Horn between Portland, Oregon, and New England, and side-wheelers began to thresh back and forth between Portland and San Francisco.

The middle sixties found Portland with a population of some 4,000 souls—half of which was transient.

Now the incoming transient, en route to or from the gold fields, had no time to make contacts with the fixed population, had he been so inclined. He craved fiercer and more stimulating entertainment than was offered in the churches or in the meetings of the Washingtonian Society—remembering the colorful pitfalls of San Francisco. The traders of Portland were practical men. They had come to Portland with the intention of furnishing the people of the West such things as they seemed to require.

"Give the customer what he wants," was their early, simple and eminently practical policy.

So they set themselves to see that the demands for new commodities should be supplied to the sweeping, transient population—a population that remembered San Francisco and Spain and New Orleans and Vienna and London and Pekin and countless other places, and that did not remember New England.

There arose saloons that were far more sinful than the one-billiard-table establishment of Jim Fruiht and Donald Stewart. There were hurdy-gurdy houses and dance halls and temples of Aphrodite that far overshadowed the simple efforts at disorderliness that poor old Madame Hamilton brought up from San Francisco a decade before. Satan claimed the transient population for his own.

The traders sold supplies to all, and collected
their rents and prospered. The permanent, Puritan population sighed as it watched the Baby-
lonian revelry of the abandoned customers—and
remained firm in the faith.

Long since have the outlines of those early
trader kings who succeeded the dynasty of Hudson's Bay and who held the whole fabric of this
dual civilization in their practical efficient hands,
blurred under the smudging of tradition. Their
patriarchal care for the spiritual and intellectual
and moral welfare of the permanent community;
their ruthless vigor and resourcefulness, the heroic
gestures with which they made and broke things
and men in colossal battles for possession of the
teeming resources of the new land; their virtues
and their vices; their huge hacking strokes in the
rough-hewing of a commonwealth after their own
individualistic ideas and ideals—most of this has
been faded into colorlessness by writers who wrote
too mildly, and by tradition mongers who talked
too gross improbabilities.

Their figures in history have already become
wax-work exhibits of long bearded gentlemen,
with hands thrust in fine nobility in the bosom
of their Prince Alberts, and a uniform expression of high idealism graved upon their respective brows. The turfs torn up in their struggles
with the construction of the new commonwealth
have healed over, and the third and fourth generations have achieved the suavity of manner that
comes with the habit of aristocracy, after the first

primeval barons have finished hacking and hew-
ing and swashbuckling and laying the broad
foundations.

This study, however, is not directly concerned
with reconstructing the personalities of the late
H. W. Corbett, William S. Ladd, Josiah Failing,
John Ainsworth and those other ·gorgeous old
individualists who came around the Horn or across
the plains seventy odd years ago and established
the dynasties that still rule Portland. They belong in the picture only as a background along
with the other fundamental elements, against
which is seen the pageant of evolving frontier
society, passing in noise and motley and gradually
losing vividness and picturesqueness and becoming
—what shall be dealt with in due season.

There was neither rail nor telegraph connection with the East. All that came and went must
come and go mainly around the Horn and through
and under the hands of the early traders. These
by virtue of their position became not only traders,
but bankers and financiers and promoters, without whose moral and money support nothing
might go forward in the new land. Thus the
early baronies were founded and grew. With
them grew Portland, filled with the dual qualities
of sin and sanctity which dwelt and functioned
side by side, with little or no friction.

Year after year the theologically controversial
capitalist found larger and larger markets for
strictly non-theological goods. In the '60's there
were the miners roaring for hard pleasures. In

the '70's sprang up the grain trade between Portland and Liverpool—with the inevitable corollary of influxes of British capital and its dual contribution of staid Scotch and British branch offices here, and wandering and wastrel adventurers of the "remittance man" type. River traffic grew on the Columbia River, almost as in the lively steamboat days on the Mississippi. Railways began to throw out their organic filaments.

All these elements brought still more of the transient, primitive, constructive type of human being that flourishes in lands that are in the newer processes of civilizing. The sailors, and the rivermen, and the construction men were simple and direct in their desires, as had been the miners before them—and there came to Portland those who can cater to the simple and direct desires of sailors, and rivermen and construction savages.

They leased room for their businesses from the Founders and possessors, and Portland continued to be the trading point of the Northwest in which the transient traveler could buy whatever he might desire or require. The trader-possessors collected their rents, and prospered, building more churches and founding schools, guaranteeing for their children and their children's children the cultural and moral advantages that properly belong to children of a community reared in the tradition of righteousness and a respect for learning.

Like Roman matrons of old, the matrons of the permanent population wrapped serenely around them the toga praetexta. They went unruffled about their life, ministering to their families, meeting their church and social duties, pondering at one time if it would not be best to organize a "New England Society" to insure the preservation of the social lines of the earlier families against obliteration by the inpouring tide of immigration that ran back to Ohio and Pennsylvania and Missouri instead of to New England.

Their contact with the shifting transient trading life that swirled parallel to their ordered community life, was the slightest. It was not especially good form to pay attention to it.

Now added upon the deep sea sailormen who rolled in on the lime juicers, and upon the hard drinking, hard playing rivermen and the miners and engineers, came the "heathen Chinee," for railroad building was in its earliest boom. With high hearts the Western communities saw the railroads coming, and since most of the effort of white men was engaged in land clearing and settlement, they viewed without great alarm the importation of thousands of coolie gangs from China. Chinatown came into existence in Portland, lying like a colorful dragon for half a mile between the shopping district along First Street and the district in which the sailors, and rivermen and gamblers and priestesses of Aphrodite moved.

The trader's and building owner's task of supplying the transient visitor with what the transient visitor required in addition to grub, picks and pack saddles, made it inevitable that in time the bartender, the gambling house proprietor, the mas-

ter of the sailor's boarding house, the business
agent of Venus, should become part of the permanent roll of inhabitants of Portland.

They belonged unquestionably to The Adversary. But they were responsible about rent and
taxes, and were practically indispensable in the
business of purveying to the transient customers
the social commodities they required. So the
traders continued to collect their rents and prosper, the permanent camp of Satan quietly increased in numbers, and the sinners and the sanctified dwelt in the ineffable peace of non-contact
(except through the ledgers), with the buffer
community of Chinatown lying between them.

The soldiers of the Lord did not lack activity
nor vigilance in those days, but their method of
attack simply was different from the method employed by the forces of righteousness to-day. The
heresy of redemption through change of environment, had not yet arisen. Satan's City of
Destruction was not disturbed. Whosoever was
naughty enough to prefer it, knew precisely
where it was and how to get there and the probable
cost of the round trip.

The movements that would be classified as
"Uplift" were reserved mainly for the permanent
community—with the exception of the forlorn
forays into the bad lands, under organizations
such as the Salvation Army.

Even these were not, in those days, as they are
to-day.

Recently Mr. and Mrs. Leslie E. Morningstar

brought out a pocket booklet of "Snapshots of
Portland History"—a most delectable volume—
in which we find jostling one another on the
page:

"April 18, 1874—Forty-six temperance workers
arrested for praying and singing on the sidewalk.

"January 18, 1876—Chief Lappens collects
quarterly license from 71 saloons, $50 each."

Most of the temperance work and its allied
works in Portland of the early seventies, was devoted to the proper training and pledge signing
by the youth of the permanent community, and
business and morality continued to be able to
thrive comfortably, side by side, with evil. But
the City of Destruction inevitably grew in its
permanent population to a stage where it made
itself felt in politics. In the early seventies, the
long line of responsible and pew-holding officials
began to be broken by officials from the side of
The Adversary.

Thomas J. Holmes was elected mayor; the
first time, according to traditionalists, that the
strength of the Adversary became apparent as a
dangerous thing to the community. With a magnificent swipe of pure romantic poetry, tradition
further says that Holmes died on the night of
his successful election, following or during celebration of his victory.

The history of Portland during the remainder
of the century is the history of how the City of
Destruction, the old "North End," dominated the
politics of Portland and of Oregon—for the rest

of the state in those days had just sufficient strength to be a likely pawn in the political games of the big personalities who wrought in the metropolis.

After the positive entry of the forces of evil into the politics of the city, there came a closer division of the sheep from the goats, and that district emerged which has since that time been know as "The North End," and designated otherwise as "the bad lands" by the gamblers; "the Big Eddy" by hobo loggers who circled around it in between jobs; and "the vice district" by the social workers, who emerged, by the way, long after it had in reality ceased to exist as a restricted district.

Its rise and evolution are not without their sardonic features. Business began to press in upon the district occupied by the crib houses around Yamhill and Taylor streets. It became apparent not only from business policy, but also from the increasing protests of the Roman matrons against the necessity of having to behold vice ungirdled and abandoned, as they were walking to and from church or prayer-meeting, also near Taylor and Yamhill, that the girls must seek another workshop.

Two practical business men, one of whom has since passed to the bosom of his fathers, foreseeing the change, decided to control it so that it should not be entirely in vain, from a business viewpoint. They leased from one of the Founders, the block at Fourth and Flanders—situate more

nearly in the heart of the sailor boarding house
and transient district—and erected thereupon
fully equipped and ready for occupancy a home
for these wandering sirens. Then they lobbied
through the city council, by the brief and efficient
golden method in vogue in those days, the ordinance that commanded the women of Babylon, in
the interests of higher morality to depart.

The girls were ready when the command came
forth and, picking up their already packed carpet
bags, migrated. The City of Destruction became
more compact and consolidated, business occupied
the ground vacated by the migrating scarlet
women, the sailors and miners had their girls, the
eyes of morality were not offended by the vision
of diademed priestesses of Aphrodite leaning
upon the cushions at their windows, and all was
serene.

Two phrases recur anent those mythical days,
from the lips of men who lived through them and
still remember them without prejudice:

"The men who controlled things in those days
believed, to paraphrase a later utterance, in
'Open-vice, openly arrived at.' "

"In those days everybody knew where he belonged and he went there and stayed there."

Although there was in those days no lack of
revivals and campaigns, and prayers and exhorta-
tions against Babylon from the pulpits in the old
town, the hosts never did get around to the actual
point of marching against the citadel of Satan
in the North End, because of his useful voting

power and practical efficiency system of handling votes at $2.50 per head. The Adversary was permitted to grow and prosper, and to pay his rent regularly to the holders of the land on which his sinful palaces were reared.

Most important and most powerful among the angels of Lucifer were the proprietors of the sailor boarding houses in the seventies and eighties. Out of them and their organizations control of the other branches of the North End life eventually emerged. The most famed and efficient of them were known, like Jim Turk, in all the seven seas. Two hundred and twenty-five pounds of florid-faced, beef-fed Britisher, with a voice like a fog horn, a hard fighter and a great bluffer, and a man who knew the hearts of sailormen, Jim Turk kinged it in the North End until his death.

In the latter years of his reign rose up yet other sailor boarding house men, as shrewd and hard fighting and practical, loved by the ship captains who shared the split with them, cursed by the owners in England, who had to foot the bill for stolen crews and ship delays, accepted by the professional sailor men as part of the process of life, bogey men for farm hands and small townsmen from up-state, and for miners and cowboys who found their excursions into the bad lands considerably cramped by the possibility that they might wake up on the other side of the Columbia bar with a brown taste in the mouth and a bruise on the skull and nothing to do but enter a year's

apprenticeship in seafaring under the belaying-
pin of a British second mate who knew how to
break men to his will. Shanghaied homesteaders
sent them cordially to hell from Bergen and
Singapore, from Cape Town and St. John's,
while Enoch Arden widows mourned them and
others worked their claims.

Bridget Grant and her husband came around
from Boston, Massachusetts, and brought another
phase of New England method to the West,
when they opened a sailor boarding house in
Astoria. Grant himself died ere many years, but
his widow efficiently carried on, and trained a
brood of tall sons in the business of sailor boarding house management. In time she graduated
them to achieve success greater even than Turk's.

When fully matured, Jack and Pete Grant
moved to the more central location in Portland
and extended the business. Astoria at the mouth
of the river—reputed in those days to be the evil-
est port in the world, and Portland, the point of
loading and unloading the cargoes for Liverpool
and Hamburg, cooperated in the business of
manipulating crews. It was part of the procedure
for the sailor-boarding house manager to put a
guard on board at Portland and send him as far
as Astoria, to make sure that none of the new
crew escaped before the ship could get to sea.

The procedure in sailor's employment was simple. When the ship came into port, the sailors
either came ashore to seek diversion after their
six months' voyage, or were persuaded to leave

the ship by a runner from the boarding houses.
On shore they were either persuaded to desert the
ship and re-ship on another, or were laid away
dead drunk pending a call for men from some
short handed ship that was ready to depart, or a
fight was started in the boarding house and when
the police arrived complaints were filed against
the visiting seamen and they were thrown into
jail.

In the latter event the captain of the ship
would wait as long as necessary and then call
upon Jim Turk, or the Grant boys or Larry Sullivan or whoever was his employment agent, and
the number of men needed would be sent out.
When the boys in jail came out again they were
ready for such employment as boarding house
keepers could get them.

It was no complaint from the regular sailors
that roused the indignation of the community
against the sailor boarding houses. Ordinarily the
sailor was a philosophical person. His idea of life
was to sail, and go ashore, and drink and riot,
and sail somewhere else and go ashore and amuse
himself again. The intricacies of business were
beyond him. He was glad to have a kindly
boarding house man attend to the detail of re-
shipping him when he had wound up his shore
leave with an empty pocket and a headache and
was ready for work again.

What brought disapproval upon the sailor
boarding house men was the roar of the cowboy
and miner and farm hand, who came down to

Portland to blow off steam and found himself
unwittingly turned into a sailor; and the howls
of the owners in England.

The Grant boys, and Mysterious Billy Smith,
and Larry Sullivan and Bunko Kelly, and the
White boys and those others in the closed corporation that controlled the boarding house business in Portland, were busy and practical men.
Some of them (like the Grants) were proud of
the fact that their passed word was sound as money
in the bank. They could not be bothered with
things outside business, like international controversies, or national or state politics.

So when James Laidlaw, the British consul, announced steps he was about to take to wipe out
the sailor boarding house evil, the Grant boys
called at his office and told him, in a matter of
fact way, that he was upsetting business and that
they would kill him if he continued to upset it.
The British consular policy was changed.

The thing that they could best understand and
deal with was the office of district attorney, and
they frankly told those who took the trouble to
ask that they didn't care a damn who might be
governor, or chief of police, or mayor or anything
else, so long as they knew where the prosecuting
attorney stood. So they faked a factional division
and no matter who was elected district attorney,
there was always one group of boarding house and
gambling house proprietors, that had supported
his campaign and made him beholden to them.

Roars or crusades had little to do with eliminating the sailor boarding houses. Changes in marine labor legislation, a temporary slump in shipping out of the Port of Portland, the disappearance of the old "lime juicers" and the rise of the steam freighters all conspired to bring a new order in which the sailor boarding house and its master had no place.

As the importance of sailor employment fell off, lumbering increased. The sailor on shore leave was replaced by the lumberjack, foot-loose with his pay check, asking only a bath, a shave, a complete new suit or woolen underwear, and from there on—all that the bartenders and ladies north of Burnside street might have to offer.

Gambling houses rose to dominance—but over them was the same ring that had controlled the sailor boarding houses. Their systemized method of controlling and delivering votes made their influence much courted by all political forces. The story of processionals of visiting sailors and loggers and section hands, voting early and often as they were marched about the North End ward, receiving $2.50 per vote per head, is one that never grows stale in the hearing. The picture of Larry Sullivan, or Bunko Kelly, or any of the other of Lucifer's archangels of the day, sitting above the ballot box with a sawed-off shotgun across the knees and keeping an eye on how the voting was done, has been preserved to us in the memory of eyewitnesses.

Long ago the Southern Pacific Railway, which came into Portland on the west side and ran the

full length of Fourth Street, to the Union Depot
beyond Hoyt, installed a station downtown. This
was partly because of convenience to the shopping
district, but chiefly, so tradition says, because the
women folk coming to Portland from the Valley
towns, objected to running the gauntlet of the
reception committee of ladies of the Bad Lands,
leaning out of their cushioned windows on either
side of Fourth Street from the time the train
passed Stark on until it reached the Union Depot.

In the height of the wide open days, the rough-
neck bars and gambling houses, "free-and-easy"
theaters and such diversion polarized around Second or Third Street and Burnside. There the
lumberjack and miner and sailor and rivermen and
visiting young experimenters from the rural communities upstate, and moralists from the small
towns who came to see how horrible it all was
and report duly to the congregations back home,
circulated and amused themselves according to
their various natures.

August Erickson's, with its six hundred foot
bar (held to be the longest bar in the world), over
which a man could buy the biggest scuttleful of
beer in the United States for a nickel, boiled with
variegated life, and there the laboring man spent
his money for wine, women and gambling according to his taste. There flourished the famous
"museum" filled with more or less Rabelaisian objects of art and curiosities. Here performed at
one time the Ladies' Orchestra, gowned in rose
pink and chastely seated within a brass railed en-

closure, the rails of which were charged with enough electricity to stop the most amorous lumberjack who might seek better acquaintance of the musicians.

Fritz's, Blaziers and a dozen others; bars and gambling tables, variety theaters where the girls took their turns on the stages and "worked the boxes," startling the visiting yokel with beer at a dollar a bottle, which he could buy downstairs for about five cents a half gallon; Bob Smith's Monte Carlo, with an orchestra playing in the ballyhoo over the street and any game you cared to try going inside. With such a catalogue one could go on indefinitely for pages. The City of Destruction flamed and blared and gamboled beyond the barrier North of Washington Street and against the buffer community of Chinatown, slopping over in spots in the form of the higher class gambling establishments and the houses of Madame Fanshawe and half a dozen other famous madames, whose histories are inextricably interwoven in the droll story of the political plots and counterplots of the time.

The Arlington club, the oldest exclusive club of the city, was on West Park Street near Alder, and diagonally across from it, enterprising sisters established a shrine to Venus, rather more elaborate and ornate than the wayside shrines north of Burnside that called the lowly lumberjack and the hard-boiled sailor. These two institutions were not mutually unaware of one another's existence, and some of the social and political history of

Portland haunts the ghosts of those buildings that have long since given way to skyscrapers.

In Madame Fanshawe's on what is now Broadway and Morrison, occupied ironically by an exclusive ladies' furnishings store, the "opium plot" developed according to testimony of the runner who turned state's evidence. It was this plot that broke Jim Lotan as collector of customs and political boss, and his conviction and fine was attended by the flight of accomplices to China to live out the remainder of their lives. Hundreds of thousands of dollars were involved in the ring, with Lotan as collector of customs heading the Portland end of it, and the smuggling ships tossing over five tael cans of opium on floats in the lower harbor for the Portland gang to pick up.

Chinatown with ten thousand or more inhabitants packed into its short stretch and ruled over by the high-binders of the day, featured prominently in the opium conspiracy. Chinatown was an unreclaimed pagan community in those days, paying its "cumshaw" to the police and bearing with oriental stoicism the working out of the white man's doctrine that John Chinaman was fair game at any and all times. It was a show place for the curious with its endlessly noisy theater, its joss house, its Harvest Festival and bonfires and banquets and periodical celebrations that carpeted the street for miles with red and yellow and green firecracker paper.

Labor in the railway construction, in the salmon canneries, in land clearing or what not, was fur-

nished by the high-binders, who controlled the
coolies with the hand of death and waxed rich
off their labors.

Tong wars still break out in the attenuated
Chinese community but they are feeble things
compared to the wars that raged in the eighties.
When a tong war broke out, the police and the
whites discreetly got off the street and left the matter in the hands of the gods of the heathen Chinee.
It reached its peak in the late eighties when one
war broke out among the rival tongs that culminated in a pitched battle in which the number
of killed and wounded has never been accurately
determined. The tong men lay in the picturesque
bannered balconies overhanging the street and all
day long the rattle of the old style Henry rifles
went on, as they enthusiastically picked off China-
men who showed in the street below, or potted
one another at long range.

Because of the firm stand of the men who controlled Portland, Chinatown escaped the catastrophe that befell the oriental quarters in cities
all along the Coast when the anti-Chinese riots
were on in the late eighties. The firmness of the
stand of the Portland leaders was partly due to
Portland's conservative attachment to the constitution and to the idea of sanctity of treaties, it is
said. But the salmon canning industry furnished
a certain incentive to diplomatic honor.

Millions in Portland capital were tied up in it,
and it was a job that in those days depended entirely upon Chinese labor. Few white men could

COURT HOUSE PARK, PORTLAND, IN THE EIGHTIES

be persuaded to undertake the bloody task of
hacking up fish all day long. There was no great
jealousy on the part of white laborers against the
fish cutters, and the big packers knew that if they
lost the "Chinks," the blow to their business would
be almost irreparable. So Portland's Chinatown
continued its colorful existence until the Exclusion Act stopped its replenishment, and then it
dwindled to its present day insignificance.

Parallel with all the merry riot of the North
End the old ordered community life outside the
Bad Lands went on. The churches grew and extended. Bridges spanned the Willamette River
and brought into the city the quiet communities
of the East Side. The railways brought from the
East a God-fearing generation of Middle Westerners. The Multnomah Amateur Athletic club
was organized with the tradition—preposterous in
those days—of having no bar in its club-house.
The tradition continues even under prohibition.

Portland had achieved a working basis under
which all types and conditions of men and women
could live satisfactorily with nothing more dis-
turbing than an occasional murder in the working
out of the feuds that necessarily developed between rival factions of gamblers and minor bosses.

An itinerant typesetter of the day who called
himself "Peter the Poet" and who used to com-
pose at the case, voiced the satirical attitude of
Oregon in general toward its fantastic metropolis
and the probability of its reform, when the Rev.
Wallace was announced coming to the city on an

evangelical mission duly equipped with a whip of
scorpions and a full quota of vials of wrath.

Sang "Peter the Poet"

> Down in Portland, Reverend Wallace
> Raised on high his holy chalice,
> Saying: "The Lord shall eat His supper
>   in this wicked river town."

Peter's poem is about all the remaining history
of the crusade of the Rev. Wallace or of others
like him who came and preached and went their
ways.

But evolution was working the change. The
sailor boarding houses were dwindled, Chinatown was fading under the Exclusion Act. The
political battles between the Ins and the Outs
in the rich fields of exploitation, and the vaulting
ambitions of the political figureheads that they
reared for banners and symbols, ultimately
destroyed the simple $2.50 per head ballot system.
Political reformers of a visionary and idealistic
turn of mind were allowed by the bosses to bring
in the Australian ballot.

Two things that came on the turn of the century helped to perfect the ruin of the strongholds
of Lucifer. Up to the early part of the century,
water boards and dock commissions and various
other organs functioning in the city, were named
by fiat of the state legislature. The fight to seize
and control these noble golden geese was waged
in the legislature by the process of putting over
from time to time a new charter, in which the

boards and commissions and what not, were distributed according to the plans and specifications of the latest faction in power. Naturally the battle concentrated around the North End in Portland, with its flexible and purchasable voting control, and politics of the state as well as the city was in a large measure fought out north of Washington street.

In the same confusion that allowed the initiative and referendum and other new-fangled devices to come in, the reform group put over a new charter, which wiped out most of the means of getting at the spoils via the legislature, and Portland city politics fell into a less dominant place in the politics of the state.

The second event was the final crash of the Mitchell machine. It came when Roosevelt, in characteristic fury over the balking of his Panama Canal plans by the games and divertissements of the railroad bloc in Congress, started to smoke out Oregon's Senator John Hipple Mitchell, who was the most serious handicap to the presidential program. In the process of Mitchell's smoking out, William J. Burns and Francis Heney uncovered the Oregon Land Frauds, and succeeded in smoking out practically everybody of any importance in Oregon.

Basically the land frauds amounted to a practice, not confined to Oregon, nor to this particular time, of staking homesteaders to prove up on government homestead and timber land, and, having gained title, to dispose of their homesteads to the big timber interests that had swarmed to Oregon from the dwindled forests of Michigan. A comparatively small number of the persons involved in the universal raid upon the public domain had the least notion that they might be engaging in something that savored of conspiracy or that might be construed as criminal. The indictment against Mitchell was largely technical.

But the whole thing filled Oregon with alarums and excursions and the crash of political thrones. Heney flamed like a meteor athwart the field. Stripling politicians who thus far had been obliged to fall into line under machine bosses, fell upon the old masters and tore them, and began carving out careers for themselves.

The war to smash the Mitchell Machine was a heroic war in which many men had been made and broken and the Oregon legislature achieved a fame for corruption that gave the world James Barton Adams' poem, so immortal that it is now generally attributed to Anonymous, "Bill's in the Legislature—but he didn't say what for."

In the progress of this war, the political reformers, typified by W. S. U'Ren, were allowed to bring in the Initiative and Referendum and the Direct Primary. The business got out of the hands of the anointed bosses and was snapped up by the lean and wily pirates of the Democratic party who were not supposed to have any rights in the state since the Civil War.

The fabric of the old order was already rent and frayed here and there when Portland decided

to hold the Lewis and Clark Centennial World's
Exposition in 1905. The old political Captains
were jaded with their mighty wars, the strength
of the old underworld had been drained somewhat
in the Klondike rush in the late nineties. Upon
this situation leaped the reformers with the necessity of cleaning house for the visitors, as a talking
point. Five of the biggest gambling houses in
the United States running wide open would not
be, they felt, the best advertisement in the world
for exposition visitors.

So they elected Tom Word sheriff on his pledge
to close the gambling houses. Tom Word was
back from Alaska and possessed certain practical
experience in dealing with hard-boiled persons in
a hard-boiled way, and a most disconcerting indifference to monetary suggestion, and Tom
Word possessed a truly Rooseveltian talent for
staging a first class show.

"I'm responsible for Multnomah county," said
Word, and inasmuch as Portland was in Multnomah county, he sent word to the Chief of Police
to clean up the gambling houses.

He was notified to go to Hell.

He sent word to the Grant boys, and August
Erickson on Burnside street, and to the Warwick
Club—most westerly outpost of Colonel Apple-
gate of Kentucky, and all the other pool halls and
gambling houses to close.

He was told unanimously to go to Hell.

So he gathered his deputies and moved upon
the Bad Lands with wagons and axes, after hav-

ing sent three warnings. Portland rocked with excitement.

George H. Williams, who as a former member of Grant's cabinet and a leading figure in Oregon, had been elected to be "Exposition Mayor," was horrified and outraged at Word's undignified methods and at Word's invasion of the Police duties of the city. He resisted with dignity but in vain. The axe campaign had captured the popular imagination.

The juries said Word was moving too soon and too fast, and turned the gambling house proprietors loose. Henry McGinn, who had grown up with the soul of Portland, said to Word:

"You are that strange and peculiar thing, a sincere and honest official, I believe. I will go down the line with you."

McGinn dug up old nuisance laws and prosecuted joyously, while Word and his men smashed doors and arrested proprietors and employees and hauled crooked wheels and faked tables and other paraphernalia up to the courthouse to be ticketed as "Exhibit A, etc." Finally the gamblers surrendered and their outfits were returned to them on their signing an agreement not to re-open their places. The stampede was on to Goldfield, Nevada, and they took their establishments to the newer and less exacting field and prospered there.

Gambling continued—discreetly under cover—the bars were ordered out of the houses in the restricted district and the girls were ordered up-

stairs and away from the windows. Portland
dropped forever between its present and its variegated past, an asbestos curtain, showing a city of
roses and homes, low taxes and undeveloped
suburban acreage, lying like a jewel amid the
emerald hills (Vid. immigration literature of the
period) with Mt. Hood, Mt. Adams, Mt. St.
Helens, lowly and individual as Fujiyama, brood-
ing in the background. Portland put on its best
clothes, told its naughty children to stay in the
background and keep their noses clean—and welcomed the world to the Lewis and Clark Centennial Exposition.

From as far as railway tourist rates extended,
America east of the Rocky Mountains sent its
emissaries. They bore back home with them reports of a land flowing with the milk and honey
of undeveloped lands, and blest with taxes so low
as to be almost unbelievably light.

The rush came on. Cow pastures that had
lingered forlornly full of buttercups on the fringes
of the city, began the cellular divisions that pre-
saged new additions. The home owner of moderate means increased by thousands and tens of
thousands. There was talk about the iniquities
of the paving trust.

Old Portland sank gurgling under the herded
and multiplied population of innumerable eastern
small towns. It was the day of the real estate
promoter.

Efficiency and luncheon clubs appeared. Social
workers began to worry about the environment of

the lumberjack and yegg. The bewildered remnants of the old army of Lucifer, broken and leaderless, and deriving no reinforcement from the new tide of immigration, dumbly beheld the coming of the end.

Harry Lane, later Senator from Oregon, came into the mayorality with reform backing, and with a burning and bitter enmity against the folk of Babylon, for both the gambling and the red light district had struck blows close to his naked heart. Another vigorous, eccentric character, he pounced upon his enemies as picturesquely and petrifically as Word had pounced upon the open gambling. The restricted district had never had any legal standing in the community, existing only by common consent and public policy of its day. So it shattered, and the daughters of Aphrodite scattered like spilled quicksilver among the hotels, apartment houses and rooming houses of the city, where they continued their calling under such precarious and temporary protection as they could afford.

There remained openly still only the saloons, feudal adherents of the big brewing interests that had grown up with the city and already their hour was drawing near. The state at large went dry under local option, long before an effective move was made on the citadels of Portland, for Oregon consisted of many comparatively small towns, in which Satan was never allowed much consideration. Portland was looked upon not only as the banker and trader, but as the restricted district

for the state at large, and so long as there was
Portland to flee to, substantial citizens of the
smaller communities—if they were not conscien-
tiously for prohibition—were, for the most part,
quite willing to drive the devil out of their own
door yards.

The last of the mayors whose type savored at
all of the old régime was A. G. Rushlight, who
came into power around 1910—and came in with
a wholesome fear of what the reform forces and
the puritan thought of the community might do
to him and his adherents.

There was clamor for a new charter on the
Commission plan instead of the Aldermanic, and
he sought to forestall it by naming a charter
revision committee of his own. A citizens' charter
committee was formed and while the Mayor's and
the citizens' committees hacked away at the body
of the old charter, various other charter specialists
came in with extra suggestions. It became apparent that a compromise commission charter
would be voted by the people—and it was very
apparent that the first commission named under
such a charter would have to have its skirts entirely clean of the stain of the old North End.

Rushlight with forlorn hope appointed a vice
commission, which deliberated and duly published
a report viewing with alarm the parlous condition
of public morals. A full page map, with the street
lines carefully erased, showed in variegated dots,
the relative location of apartment houses, hotels,
rooming houses and what not, in which the daugh-

ters of Aphrodite had sought sanctuary from the besom of Lane. An hour after the report was published, draughtsmen in most of the architects' offices around town had reconstructed the streets on the map.

Portland guffawed and gobbled up the reports as fast as it could lay hands on them, and rules and compasses and dividers had a momentary boom on the market. One of the leading concerns in the city, having to do with building administration and rentals, emerged roaring for the scalp of the Mayor and threatening damage suits by the score, because the committee report had plastered red spots on the majority of apartment houses under that company's jurisdiction.

It was Satan's fatal fiasco. The commission form of government came in and Rushlight was hoisted out. Under H. R. Albee as Mayor, came in a commission against no member of which the god-fearing and law-upholding element of the city could protest. The memorable event in Albee's administration having any bearing on this study of social evolution, was the enactment of the "Tinplate Ordinance." This required that the name of the owner of any building used as a hotel, rooming or lodging house, should be displayed on the building on a tin plate of such and such size. It was imagined that in some mystic way it would be possible to pin the responsibility for lurking sirens upon the ultimate consumer of the rental for the building.

With a feeling of chilled horror, old established

families and trust companies found what to them amounted to The Scarlet Letter, pinned upon the bosom of their most remunerative properties, while the peasantry smacked its thighs and roared with throaty mirth. But the novelty wore off and the joke slumbered, and it is doubtful if anyone gives more than passing notice to the tin plates on the lodging houses, hotels, apartment houses and rooming houses—even if they should see the patrol wagon drawn up in front of them, while the Police carry out a trunk of moonshine or a still or a couple of experimenters in life against whom the next flat has complained.

In the first election under the commission charter, George L. Baker, a theater man who had figured in the city council since the early part of the new century, wistfully saw the collapse of all the campaigning methods that he had learned in his political career thus far.

Unlike many of his confreres, he was willing to learn his lesson and wherever necessary to fall in line with the newer tendencies insofar as he could understand them. How far he was able to do this is perhaps best indicated by the fact that he came back into power as Mayor, in the election which with a slight reaction against the sincere, churchly and somewhat colorless administration of Albee returned that gentleman to private life. It was this election also that resulted in a realignment of the city commission.

The half century fight for woman suffrage, which was long waged almost single-handed by

Abigail Scott Duniway, the sister of Harvey W. Scott, flowered at last in victory.

While the politicians, still groggy from the other blows they had received, were trying to find out just where they stood and what they might expect from the new voting element, state prohibition crashed in and demolished the wheezy remnants of the battered old political machine of the North End.

Then politics went into a gibbering panic, and since those fateful years, practical politicians have been burning punk sticks before what they refer to as "the church element," and consulting oracles and installing dictaphones in a bewildered effort to guess what the churches and the Y. M. C. A. and the Anti-Saloon League and the League of Women Voters demand of them in return for continuance in the public service. Mayor Baker has done the best guessing thus far, it would seem, although one or two who took their training in the old school have come unobtrusively back into the city hall, without their checked suits.

One guess is perhaps as good as another. Probably the reason Mayor Baker seems to have done the best guessing is because he loves to be Mayor for the sake of being Mayor, because with all his practical political craft he registers sincerity, he sincerely loves Portland and believes in Portland and desires to make Portland a city of a million inhabitants. He might, if permitted to work steadily at the job of being Mayor (instead of having to hop into his dinted armor at a moment's

notice to defend his political existence almost
every day), accomplish something of the ingenu-
ous dream which he appears to cherish.

But this is not permitted him. His life becomes
a long series of heroic sallies in defense of his political life. A breathless interval in which he can
consider the needs and welfare of the city he loves
to reign over as Mayor—and in dashes a mes-
senger with news that Birnam Wood is on the
move again, and the Macduff is jimmying his way
in at the side window of the city hall, or that Mal-
colm has just called the young warriors to a council at the City Club, with a view to bringing about
the delayed supper of which Peter the Poet sang.
Out sword, up buckler and storm to the battle-
ments, cursing the witches!

In his later battling, Mayor Baker has, unwittingly perhaps, pinned his faith almost entirely
upon the formula that the old Founders found
so effective and profitable in the beginning of
things:

"Give the customer what he says he wants."

It seems to be a good formula.

It has not been many weeks since Mayor Baker
responded to a toast at a luncheon of the Minis-
terial Association at the Y. M. C. A.

He towered ruggedly at the head of the table,
a giant of a man with a look of profoundest
earnestness struggling with a look of puzzled
distress upon his face.

"You see before you," he said, "a man who not
many years ago had very little respect for the so-

called 'better element' of the city and who felt a sort of contempt for them and the things they seemed to be trying to do.

"You see before you to-day, a man who has the profoundest respect and admiration for this better element. You have said that you want Portland to be made a clean, law-abiding, upright community, and I am here to serve you with what ability I have."

The association applauded roundly.

Not long after the newspapers announced with enthusiasm that Mayor Baker ceremoniously in the presence of the assembled ladies of the W. C. T. U. had signed the pledge.

Portland is back on her stride. For years now the politics of city and state have been as rich in theological implications as those of the physically ancestral New England or the spiritually ancestral Palestine of the prophets. Portland of the early '50's scarcely took such issues more seriously.

And now, at the behest of the regenerated Mayor Baker and of the Portland Ad Club seeking regeneration yet more concentrated, the Rev. Dr. William A. Sunday is scheduled for a revival campaign in the fall of 1925. That left hand of Portland which did for so long what its right hand did not deign to notice officially, is due in its withered state for amputation and the last public impalement of shame.

Also,—among his other array of related exhibits,

the reverend visitor will enter a Hereford bull at the livestock show.

After all, even in saved Portland, these are the 1920's. So even in the stride of sanctity regained lingers the faint, irredeemable tempo of jazz.

KANSAS CITY:

HOUN' DAWG VS. ART
By
Henry J. Haskell

KANSAS CITY

I TRUST I am a person of proper sensibilities. So it is with a fitting sense of shame and humiliation that I here record the fact that Kansas City of to-day, tamed, domesticated, Kiwanized, Chamber-of-Commerced, Heart-of-Americaed as it is, with the issue of its civilization still in the balance, nevertheless to me is more desirable, more interesting in every way than the bold, bad town that outfitted the Santa Fe and Oregon trade, the Pikes-Peak-or-Bust rush, and the cow country, and that grew maudlin in the House of Lords bar when it chanted the lament over the death of its hero:

Jesse James was a lad that killed a-many a man;
He robbed the Danville train.
But that dirty little coward that shot Mr. Howard
Has laid poor Jesse in his grave.

It was Robert Ford that dirty little coward,
I wonder how he does feel.
For he ate of Jesse's bread and he slept in Jesse's bed,
Then laid poor Jesse in his grave.

Jesse was a man, a friend to the poor,
He never would see a man suffer pain;
And with his brother Frank, he robbed the Chicago bank,
And stopped the Glendale train.

I recognize this preference for the modern city as a weakness, and I do not boast of it. Perhaps it is due to unfortunate early training. For I distinctly recollect that when I arrived in Kansas City many years ago I was quite unable to share in the enthusiasm of many of the older inhabitants for Jesse James, Jr., who was on trial on a charge of train robbery. Not that I was prejudiced against the son of the unlucky victim of the gentleman who shot Mr. Howard. He was acquitted. But I did not take easily to the fact that many reputable citizens were evidently less concerned in the evidence of his innocence than in the circumstance that he was the son of the border Robin Hood. A chip of the old block, by gad, sir!

It may be, too, that the town of the early days lacked some of the picturesqueness that belongs by tradition to a frontier community. It never was scalped by Indians, shot up by cow punchers, or debauched by prospectors with their pockets full of gold nuggets. Joseph Smith and his followers settled on its outskirts and might have contributed variety to its life. But the settlers rose against the Mormons and they sought refuge elsewhere. The river trade offered possibilities. But the railroads choked it off. With their development in the '60's the frontier rapidly retreated westward. It had hardly restrained long enough to be seriously lamented. One day it was there. Next day Kansas City organized a Chamber of Commerce and lined up with the coming industrial age. It is difficult to yearn backward after one's great-grand-aunt who only lived ten minutes.

In the '70's the city's only real frontier asset

was a legacy from border warfare days, the James gang. When Governor Crittenden invited political ruin by offering a reward for Jesse with unexpectedly successful results, as the ballad of the dirty little coward testifies, the community at the Kaw's mouth was definitely turned toward standardization. Its traditions were broken.

The place was never even a typical cow town. By the time the big demand for beef cattle came, after the war, the railroads were tapping the range to the west of the Missouri. The great herds from Texas that were driven north over the Chisholm and other trails, reached rail transportation first at Abilene, Kansas, and then at Dodge and Ogalalla. Those were the centers of cowpuncher life. It was at Dodge, not at Kansas City, that Boots Hill cemetery was established for the convenient disposal of the gentlemen who died with their boots on. The cattle were shipped from those railroad points to farmers further east or to the stockyards at Kansas City and Chicago. A few herdsmen rode the trains with them and gave a cow country atmosphere to the hotels, eating houses and saloons near the stockyards. But the boys with the high heel boots, chaps and spurs, were undeniably exotic in Kansas City. They were swallowed up in the larger life of the community which was busy killing hogs, handling wheat, grinding flour, and supplying agricultural implements to the grain farmers.

The city, as I just said, was on the road to a standardization of the commonplace commercial

type. From that catastrophe it was saved by
Providence or a fortuitous concourse of atoms.
Its placid progress was suddenly disturbed by a
volcanic eruption. A bulky middle-aged man
from Indiana came storming into town. After
that it was never the same.

Two things, I suppose, made Kansas City—the
Great Bend of the Missouri and Nelson of The
Star. The Bend requires more explanation than
Nelson. Its importance is less obvious. The Missouri sweeps down from the north past Omaha,
St. Joe, Atchison, and Leavenworth. At the
junction with the Kaw, more politely known as
the Kansas, it turns abruptly to the east and goes
swirling across the state to meet the Mississippi
just above St. Louis.

You see? Probably not. To the present generation inland water transportation does not exist.
But the outfitters for the overland trade, bucking
the muddy current on the Felix X. Aubrey, the
Cataract, the Sultan, the Silver Heels, the Star of
the West, and other famous steamers, sought the
maximum cheap water haul to the west. Where
the up-river boats turned north goods were taken
ashore for the long trek. That meant a trading
post at the mouth of the Kaw where the overland
trails whipped out their ribbons toward Oregon
and Santa Fe.

So the trading post developed with many vicis-
situdes into an outfitting point and later a distributing center. Until the eruption of 1880 it was

distinguished only for its energy and a self confidence that was its real religion. William Rockhill Nelson, the erupter, was a huge man, short of leg but enormous of frame. Julian Street wrote of him in his later years that he was more like a volcano than any other man he had ever met; mountainous in his proportions and also in the way he tapered up from his vast waist to his snow capped peak, with a Vesuvian voice, hoarse, deep, rumbling, strong. "When he speaks," Street wrote, "great natural forces seem to stir, and you hope no eruption may occur while you are near, lest the fire from the mountains descend upon you and destroy you." The eruptions escaped from under a long, quivering upper lip and were reinforced by slaps with a heavy hand on the desk. They welled up from a temperament that was a combination of Lorenzo the Magnificent and Jim Hill, with a dash of St. Francis, Nietzsche, and Oliver Cromwell. Wherever Fate happened to plant Nelson he hoisted his flag and took charge. He took charge of the unkempt town where he printed his paper. It struggled, but it could not escape.

A late photograph shows him seated with a huge hand in the foreground. "That paw is not overemphasized," a stranger remarked, happening on the picture after visiting Kansas City. "It is all over the place."

Nelson was of British stock. The family had been in America since the seventeenth century. But for all his Anglo-Saxon aggressiveness he was the embodiment of the Latin civilization which is the civilization of beauty. Instinctively he regarded the industrialism of his day with the same abhorrence that France feels toward the monstrous industrial organization that is Germany. He might not have admitted it, but he had the Gallic apprehension that this terrible machine would some day come rolling down and destroy everything that made life worth while.

"Don't talk to me about a campaign to bring factories to Kansas City," he exclaimed one day to a delegation of town boosters. "A city isn't made by bringing in a horde of cheap laborers to make cotton prints. Put on a campaign for an art gallery and I'm with you."

So for thirty-five years, by sheer strength of a dominating will he sought to impose the things of the spirit on a chronically dismayed trading community which habitually resented but could not evade his dictation. Kansas City is not to be understood without understanding the long struggle between the frontier town of the stockyards, the checker board mud streets, and the Boston store, and this outsider, who without knowing it, was the incarnation of an alien outlook on life.

Returning to the physical basis of things, I have said it was the Great Bend of the Missouri that determined that a city should exist at this particular point. It was the advance of the ice sheet that made the Great Bend. Every spring the melting ice poured out flood waters from its fringes. These plowed a wide channel from the northwest to the south and east in which the shrunken Missouri still flows, the mere remnant of a once mighty stream. The southwestern extremity of the ice sheet covered northeastern Kansas. Around the glacier's giant elbow swept the Missouri in its great bend to the east.

Settlements clustered up and down the river at this strategic point. On the North side Kentucky settlers organized a county and named it for their hero, Clay, with Liberty as its county seat. On the south side settlers from Virginia called their county for the rival hero, Jackson, and named the county seat equally for the rights of man, Independence. Up stream appeared Leavenworth, Atchison, St. Joe, Council Bluffs. The river towns became competitors for the Santa Fe trade that began in the '30's and the Oregon trade that started in the next decade. Early in the century French fur traders from St. Louis had established a trading post at the mouth of the Kaw. When the steamboats began coming up the river with goods for Santa Fe they discovered the best landing place by Chouteau's warehouse at the foot of what is now Main Street, Kansas City. Traders found it convenient to route their stuff by Chouteau's landing and haul it over a trail made by a ravine to the main Santa Fe trail at the little hamlet of Westport that had sprung up on the trail a few miles west of Independence. A settlement developed at the landing and spread back on the plateau behind the river bluffs. There in a tavern adjoining Colonel Titus's palatial three-story gambling house, a meeting was held presided over by One-Eyed Ellis, who made his living selling bad whiskey to the Indians, and the settlement was christened the Town of Kanzas. Later it became City of Kansas, and only within a generation Kansas City.

An Eastern newspaper man, Albert D. Richardson, visiting the place in 1857 on a journey through the West, tells of the steamboat port with its "immense piles of freight, horses, ox and mule teams receiving merchandise from steamers, scores of immigrant wagons and a busy crowd of whites, Indians, half-breeds, negroes and Mexicans. Carts and horses wallowed in the mud. Drinking saloons abounded and everything wore the accidental, transitory look of new settlements." But the people had the characteristic spirit of the pioneers which is incarnate today in the town booster clubs of the West.

"There was much stir and vitality," says Richardson, "and the population, numbering two thousand, had unbounded, unquestioning faith that here was the city of the future."

In the inevitable race for commercial supremacy Independence, Leavenworth, and St. Joe for a time were in the lead. Then Fate loaded the dice and rolled them for the Landing at the Great Bend of the Missouri. The railroads discovered the water level grades converged at the mouth of the Kaw. Take a freight car two hundred miles to the northwest, west, or southwest of that

KANSAS CITY IN 1855

strategic point, give it a shove, and it will coast down to Kansas City. That fact determined the location of the future distributing center.

Eighteen fifty-seven was the highwatermark of the old river port and outfitting post. It is recorded that fifteen hundred steamboat landings were made that year. Then the border troubles and the war swept over the town and left only débris. The overland trade, interrupted by raiders, was diverted to Fort Leavenworth where the government garrison offered protection. The City of Kansas withered. It was held by Union troops through the war, but most of the country about it had been settled from the South and was Secessionist in sympathy. Bands of marauders were organized in Missouri to raid Eastern Kansas, and other bands of marauding Kansans raided back. It was all done in the name of patriotism. To-day there are reputable families in Jackson County who still have Kansas loot, and a Kansas friend tells me that the piano in the old home near Lawrence was stolen from a Missouri farm house. The newspapers carried almost daily announcements that Major Long had killed six bush-whackers beyond Independence and burned three farm houses, and that Captain Liggett had captured three Union soldiers outside Kansas City, cut off their ears and hung them to a tree. These barbarities culminated in Quantrell's raid on Lawrence in 1863 in which one hundred and fifty men of the town were killed. The bushwhackers were sheltered by Southern sympathizers among the Jackson County farmers. So five days after the raid the Union commander at Kansas City, General Thomas Ewing, retaliated with the locally famous Order No. II, under which all the inhabitants of Jackson and neighboring counties, except those in a few centers, were driven from their homes. Those suspected of Southern affiliation were ordered out of Western Missouri. It was this sort of ruthlessness applied by Weyler in his reconcentrado orders against the Cuban insurrectionists that aroused America against Spain. The effect on an English-speaking population was terrific. Its results still linger more than sixty years after the event.

After the war, when the railroads began to steam out along the water levels in every direction, settlers flocked in and the town came back with a rush. But order No. II brooded over it and the community was torn in two by bitterness. The Northern crowd and the Southern crowd each developed its own social life, with separate society functions, separate churches, separate cemeteries. There are families that still caution visitors from New England not to refer to "rebels" in the presence of callers.

As for politics, the results were far reaching. The central phalanx of the Unterrified Democracy of Kansas City is made up of families with war traditions. For them to vote a Republican ticket would be to make a covenant with hell. With this phalanx the Irish, on their way up from the section hand status, made a political alliance. The combination was invincible. The Southerners furnished the party its substantial side, its respectability. The Irish were the trench workers who saw that plenty of ballots of the right sort got in the boxes even when voters were lacking, and supplied the bosses. At its best the Southern element in the post-war Kansas City represented a fine individualistic culture. At its worst it injected into the town's life the houn' dawg tradition. Neither extreme was much concerned with public improvements. Neither was possessed of that Puritan missionary spirit which wishes to establish certain standards for the rest of the community. This attitude on the part of the closely welded Democratic bloc was to affect the city's development for the next half century.

In the boom that followed Appomattox, Kansas City had one short, sharp struggle with its vigorous rival, Leavenworth, over the first railroad bridge to cross the Missouri. By superior alertness and energy the town at the Kaw's mouth won. A Burlington connection crossed the river into Kansas City. It was the second through line from the East. The race between the cities ended with Kansas City far ahead.

The conditions of its settlement and growth were reflected in a joyous crudity. There it sprawled in the mud, an overgrown village with its saloons, dance halls, variety shows, its gorgeous accommodations for the transaction of keno, faro, chuck-a-luck, roulette, and stud poker, and such other arrangements as the tastes of the times required. There it sprawled, growing in size, if not in grace, until the year 1880 ushered in a new era.

Nelson, editor of a small newspaper at Fort Wayne, Indiana, surveying the human comedy as it unfolded over the continent, decided that Kansas City offered the best location for the working out of his newspaper ideas. He started The Star in the Garfield-Hancock presidential campaign. I happened to know him fairly well in his later years. But I never was really acquainted with him. Nobody was. He was always a well of undiscovered possibilities. Even to himself he must have remained a good deal of a mystery. When he reached the Kaw's mouth at the age of thirty-nine most of his possibilities were still undeveloped. Temperamentally he did not belong with the hell-roaring crowd that was dominant in the town. While he occasionally played poker with his fellow citizens, those associated with him noticed a certain aloofness. He did not quite know where he did belong. He was still trying to find himself.

He was the product of the aristocracy of a small town. His forebears had taken a hand in public affairs. They were of the elect. His grandfather Rockhill had been the first man to plant a thousand acres of corn. His father had sent him from Fort Wayne, his birth place, to the discipline of that Botany Bay for bad boys of his time, Notre Dame. He was too much of a problem for the

Fathers, and they politely passed him back to his
parents. He had made money in real estate, he
had tried planting cotton in the South after the
war, he had been a contractor, building roads and
bridges; he had been Tilden's Indiana manager,
and then, thirsting to move men in the mass, he
had tried himself out on a Fort Wayne newspaper
for a year or two. He came to Kansas City to
carve out a career, almost at middle age. His
chief resources were in his head, and in the confidence of men of means back in Indiana who were
ready to lend him money.

When I said he was a combination of Lorenzo
and several other gentlemen of mark, I was not
speaking at random. I was trying to suggest
some of the discordant elements that made him
what he was. I did not understand the Lorenzo
side of him until I had been in Florence and had
seen the sort of splendor that flamed in the soul
of the greatest of the Medicis, and that he had tried
to build into the city on the Arno. Nelson had
the same feeling for beauty and magnificence.
Like Jim Hill he was a builder with imagination. In some moods he had the altruism and
piety of St. Francis. The beauty of the worship
of the ritualistic churches appealed to him. In
other moods he could be completely agnostic, and
as ruthless and wilful as Nietzsche's superman.
One city political campaign he ruined by insisting
on pounding on a trivial side issue because it happened to be one of his whims. Yet for great
issues that won him he was willing to take any

risk. The sudden slamming of a door would make
the tears start. Yet in the face of danger he was
absolutely placid. At such times he seemed without nerves. He cried when he accidentally
stepped on a canary. But when an influential
citizen, urging him to abandon a policy that was
crushing an enemy, suggested it would be wonderful if he could go to bed thinking not a soul in
town hated him, "By God," he boomed, "I
couldn't sleep." As for the dash of Oliver, I admit the imperfection of the analogy. Cromwell
was a magnificent insurgent who finally triumphed
and himself became the sign and symbol of authority. Nelson's greatest victories, like the mil-
leniums he was constantly expecting to come
marching at his orders, were always just around
the next corner. He never transcended his insurgency.

He came to Kansas City from the small town
atmosphere. He knew he was a rebel against
authority and tradition. He knew his newspaper
must be different from any other. He knew that
ugliness and bad taste were intolerable. He knew
he was for the under dog, and he sincerely believed he was an intense democrat, not realizing
that the only democracy he could endure was that
imposed by himself as autocrat. In short he did
not understand that he was essentially a Latin
with Anglo-Saxon trimmings. Lincoln was never
his hero. He could much more readily compre-
hend Napoleon. It was by no accident that while
he was abroad he spent most of his time in Paris.

It was his spiritual home. He liked the French and was more comfortable with them than with his ancestral English. By temperament and instinct he belonged to the civilization of beauty.

That civilization was no part of the heritage of the pioneer. The medieval peasant could go out from his mud hut and help build Notre Dame of Chartres. The American pioneer often lived in a sod house, but cathedral building was not in his line. As for the town of Nelson's choice, it was very much as C. L. Edson wrote in his Ballad of Kansas City:

The herders and the traders and the sod corn crew,
They planted 'em a city when the world was new,
They planted Kansas City and the darn thing grew!

The bear cat killers and the Dan Boone clan,
The boys that taught the panther his respect for man—
They planted Kansas City where the bull trails ran.

Ships made Carthage, gold made Nome,
Grain built Babylon, the wars built Rome,
Hogs made Chicago with their dying squeal,
Up popped Pittsburgh at the birth of steel;
Come, Kansas City, make your story brief:
"Here stands a city built o' bread and beef."

Well, the herders and the traders and the sod corn crew, the bear cat killers and the Dan Boone clan in many respects are admirable. It would have been impossible to conquer the wilderness without them. There was a spirit, an *élan* about them that their successors might well cultivate. But the city they built was not distinguished for sweetness and light. They had come from the country or from small towns. Many of them expected to make their pile and move on. They were not concerned over such refinements of civilization as garbage systems or paved streets.

One day in the early eighties two Main Street merchants were standing on the wooden sidewalk, contemplating the sea of mud that was the street. One was overheard saying to the other: "You've got the worst mud hole of a town here I ever saw. Why don't you pave your street?" "Me pave it?" exclaimed the other. "Hell, I don't care if they never pave it. I live in Louisville."

A friend tells of a dinner he attended years ago at which the leading pioneer merchant was a guest. The great man complacently inspected the pictures on the walls of the living room. Coming to the Mona Lisa he stopped and looked it over carefully with hands clasped behind him. "Ah," he observed cheerfully, "the lady has a pleasant face."

In the present generation when an art commission was proposed for the city a leading alderman opposed the measure in the council. "I don't see no need of this," he said. "Art is on the bum in Kansas City."

At the time of Nelson's arrival the outlook was not glittering. The city had an adequate district of painted ladies. Its most popular theater was the Comique variety show, its most pretentious restaurant a saloon. Stores and houses were generally designed in the dry goods box style of archi-

tecture. It was a community of go-getters with
a houn' dawg background. The go-getter spirit
kept it on its toes fighting for railroads, fighting
for trade. The houn' dawg tradition left it satisfied to be stuck in the mud.

Nelson used to say it was sheer selfishness that
drove him into his never ending campaign to make
the houn' dawg town into a modern city.

"I was going to live here, wasn't I? Well, if I
ever expected to get anywhere with my paper
Kansas City had to be made into a place that
somebody besides a few dollar swappers would
want to live in. By God, it was a ground hog
case."

But it was something more than that. He could
no more help trying to shatter this sorry scheme
of things in order to re-mold it nearer to the
heart's desire than he could help breathing. He
was Restlessness incarnate. He was forever driven
by the devils within him—or the angels—to smash
and build.

Within the first year of his advent began the
long struggle to impose his alien civilization on
the raw trading post. It was a struggle that was
to last for a generation. A struggle that neither
he nor Kansas City understood at first. But as it
went forward its objects became clearer and the
struggle fiercer until both combatants were lost in
the cloud of enveloping dust, and all that came to
outside observers was the thud, thud of blows,
given and taken, the heavy breathing of Nelson,

and the screams of the angry city as each repeatedly knocked the other down and both returned to the attack. It was a lovely fight!

The new editor had realized that with the development of cheap pulp paper there was a wide and unoccupied field in the West for the two-cent newspaper. That was the sort he undertook to print in Kansas City although he had to import kegs of pennies to enable his newsboys to do business. He had an instinct for the sort of human stuff the average person likes to read; especially the average woman. ("The wife decides what paper the family will have. Let the other fellows print a paper for the men. I'm going to take care of the women.") In his newspaper the news of the world capitals was slighted. ("I'd like to read it, but there are so few of me.") It devoted itself to homely things, including the gossip necessary to humankind, and good reprint. ("Plato and Cicero and Shakespeare and Macaulay and Huxley wrote almost as good stuff as some of our modern magazine writers, you know. Why not go back occasionally and dig up some of the things they wrote?")

His own taste recognized a line of decency that must not be overstepped. A clergyman became involved in a particularly nauseous scandal. The news broke in Nelson's absence from the office. The enterprising city editor got out an extra edition with all the salacious details. The next morning when Nelson came in the editor rushed up to him for praise.

"What did you think of our extra, Mr. Nelson?" inquired the luckless one.

"I thought it was an infernal outrage that no decent newspaper would have printed and that only a damned ass would have put out."

"Well, well," exclaimed the gasping editor. "Do I understand you don't want me around here any more?"

"By God, could I make it any plainer?"

But when the town's leading merchant became involved in an affair that led to a fist fight with an enraged husband before a happy crowd at a street corner, Nelson ordered the event covered in full. Before the paper was out a lawyer stopped at The Star office.

"I have a contract here for a thousand dollars' worth of advertising," the lawyer said. Hitherto the merchant in question had disdained to advertise in the upstart newspaper. "The advertising will begin tomorrow. By the way, you won't mention that unfortunate little affair at the corner this morning, I suppose?"

"That thousand dollars looked mighty big to me," Nelson said, telling of the incident later. "But of course I knew that a newspaper that suppresses news commits suicide. So I told him I would like the contract, but we were going to print the story, and he hinted I was an unpractical person and went away."

So The Star, informal, unconventional, sprightly, refusing to sell its soul in any conspiracy of silence, won readers day by day.

Then it was that the editor, viewing the town site with an appraising eye, felt sure enough of his position to begin suggesting that certain improvements must be made. The city was in the mud. It must be paved. It had wooden sidewalks. They must be made of permanent material. Garbage was dumped in alleys and vacant lots. It must be collected and disposed of. The city was in the grasp of a horsecar monopoly. There must be cable cars. There were no shaded streets. Trees must be planted. There were no public baths. They must be built. There was no hall adequate for large gatherings. The tight-wads must be shaken down and made to build one. There were no parks and boulevards—. But here an outraged houn' dawg citizenry balked. Parks and boulevards! That was too much.

Nelson saw he was in for a real fight. He began light skirmishing until he should be so well established that his enemies could not destroy him. In the first year of The Star he mildly suggested parks. For a decade he kept talking about their desirability. He employed engineers to make studies. Then he had a bill drafted empowering the city to acquire park land. By the time it had got through the legislature the community was aroused and the battle was on. The supreme court held the new law invalid. Nelson brought his heavy artillery into action. The shrieks of the wounded resounded from the Missouri bluffs to Brush Creek and the dead filled the trenches. A charter amendment was drawn to grant the city the necessary authority. It had to be submitted to the voters and the issue was in doubt. There was a rough-neck Irish police commissioner who had fought his way up from the ranks in politics. He had a spark in him that recognized a kindred spark in the editor of The Star. A few days before the election he called at the newspaper office.

"Colonel," he inquired (for as William Allen White once remarked, Mr. Nelson always was coneliferous), "Colonel, you seem interested in that damned charter amendment."

"Why not? There isn't anything more important to Kansas City."

"I don't know as to that. I don't know much about those things. But if you want it, by God, we'll put it over for you. Don't worry."

So the People and pure Democracy scored another triumph through the medium of a benevolent autocracy. A recalcitrant and protesting city had a foreign park and boulevard system thrust upon it.

Of course I do not intend to imply that this program was put over by one man single handed. He rallied to his banner people to whom his ideas appealed. But he rode at the head of the procession and while he believed in lieutenants and used them he did not care particularly for colonels on his staff. He could supply all the necessary ideas himself and the ideas of others, unless he could at once incorporate them into his own scheme, were rather a nuisance.

One resourceful lawyer he particularly liked.

"If you want the city to undertake something that isn't exactly contemplated by the charter and the constitution and such foolishness, most lawyers spend all their time telling you how it can't possibly be done. Frank always says, 'All right, I believe we can find a way to do that.'"

With the winning of the park fight Nelson took his family to Europe. There he remained for two years. While he traveled extensively Paris was his headquarters. French he learned to read fluently. He entered into the life about him with the keenest interest. It made a profound impression on him. There he found himself. Thereafter he was explicitly a part of the civilization of beauty, as the city built on bread and beef was to discover to its increasing disturbance. When he returned home the opposition newspaper had an inspiration. It published what was ostensibly an interview with him on his travels, with all his answers to the reporter's questions translated into French.

"Did you enjoy Europe, Colonel?"

"*Mais oui, beaucoup. Très beaucoup.*"

"Is it cold in Paris in the winter?"

"*Rarement. Il y gèle, naturellement, et surtout pendant les mois de janvier et février.*"

"What do you think of Bryan?"

"*C'est un garçon comme il faut.*"

The city editor who conceived this idea was nearer right than he knew. Superficially Nelson had not changed. He still cherished an almost

fanatical adoration of Kansas City. But whether
he realized it or not—and probably he did not allow himself to realize it—he returned from Europe
more than ever a spiritual alien to the go-getter
and houn' dawg atmosphere that still pervaded
Main Street, Walnut Street, Grand Avenue and
the packing centers of the West Bottoms.

In Europe he had become interested in painting.
How interested was demonstrated in the final disposition of his estate to which I shall refer later.
He brought home with him the nucleus of an art
collection—a large number of excellent copies of
Old Masters, which he felt would be better than
the few inferior originals that were available.
These he gave to the city with the proviso then
necessary that the collection should be open to the
public on Sundays as well as other days.

He had built for himself a home, a delightful
rambling old English country house of native
stone, covered with ivy. He acquired a large tract
of land about it and set out to provide an example
in town planning. He put winding roads through
the tract, lined them with stone walls, planted
rambler roses along the walls, set out trees, and
used shrubbery in such masses as never had been
seen west of the Hudson. Houses he built from
his own design by the score; houses of modest cost
to demonstrate that a small house need not be
ugly. The English country side had appealed especially to him. His district might have been part
of an English village. The Baron of Brush Creek,
the town called him, after a stream that ran

through the domain, and people said not inappropriately that he was a feudal lord living among his tenantry.

As his newspaper developed and his power grew and his purposes crystalized he became increasingly autocratic. He was going to make Kansas City over or know the reason why. Unluckily for his immediate success his social and political insurgency blossomed so that his program for justice alienated the wealthy and cultured part of the community that was naturally with him in his program for beauty. His policies forced a go-getter houn' dawg coalition that was vigorous and bitter. Besides, people resented being constantly told what they ought to do and being driven with a club to do it. In his later years Nelson's pet plans were mostly bowled over when the people got a chance at them. They might really approve of some project for beautification, but they didn't propose to have it choked down their throats. Not if they knew it.

In that era of revolt against what was commonly called Nelsonism, the property owning class, with pretty general approval, might have put its case against Star dictation in about this fashion:

Under the malign direction of Nelson The Star has kept things constantly stirred up. It has made tenants dissatisfied. They never used to complain about light and air. Now they won't look at a house unless every window opens on a flower garden with a humming bird in it. The Star won't let anybody alone. It insists on regulating the

minutest detail of people's lives. Its regulations
are pernicious and extravagant. Its preaching
about more parks and boulevards and breathing
spaces and supervised playgrounds for children,
and plant Dorothy Perkins roses, and swat the
fly, and housing reform, and a new charter, and
art galleries, and keep your lawn trimmed, and
take a lot of baths, and throw out the bosses, and
use the river, and cut the weeds on vacant lots,
and read the Home University Library, and for
God's sake don't build such ugly houses, and make
the landlord cut a window in the bath room, and
put goats in Swope Park, and why will mothers
risk their babies' lives by bringing them up on
bottles, and plant your bulbs now, and teach your
children manners, and what's the use of lawyers,
and cultivate a pleasant speaking voice, and build
a civic center, and put out houses for the birds,
and walk two miles before breakfast, and why are
Pullman cars so hot in winter, and go to church,
and cut out the children's adenoids, and build trafficways, and sleep with your windows open, and
the square deal, and build cyclone-proof houses,
and smash the saloons, and pooh, pooh, on factories that employ women, and reduce street car
fares, and go look at Old Masters every Sunday,
and use two by sixes instead of two by fours if
you want your house to stand up, and move out in
the suburbs, and tear down the tin bridges and
build hard surface roads everywhere, and all the
other things, has increased the cost of living and

given people inflated ideas, and pretty nearly ruined the town.

That was about the position of the element that was in chronic rebellion against the Nelson dictatorship of the later years. There was constant turmoil. Nelson fumed and fought and Kansas City fumed and fought back. But it was at a disadvantage. It couldn't get away from the editor. He went into every house in town twice a day— the greatest bargain in good reading, he used to boast, to be found anywhere on the globe; thirteen papers for ten cents a week; now is the time to subscribe! People may be careless readers or hostile readers. But if they keep on reading day after day, year after year, some of the ideas are bound to sink in.

When Nelson died in 1915 after thirty-five years of storming at the stupid ugliness of things, he had appreciably changed the current of life in Kansas City. Without him it might have been simply another—well, say, Omaha.

This sounds a reckless statement. It may properly be asked whether after all any one man could appreciably affect the life of a whole community—whether eventually the current would not swing back into the old channel. Is not Kansas City essentially the same as the other mid-Western Zeniths, with hotels after Statler, stores after Lord and Taylor, clubs after Rotary, activities regulated by the Chamber of Commerce, with a slogan, Kansas City Heart of America, which it felt

should determine the arrangement of the flowers
it sent to President Harding's funeral? In the
taming process has it not lost the picturesqueness
of the days of the old overland freighters and become a commonplace, hustling, uninspired commercial center like a score of others?

Fair questions. Still, the characteristics I have
catalogued are rather superficial. Standardization, I take it, is not in itself necessarily objectionable. It is objectionable when it is an outward
symbol of an inward dullness. It is objectionable
when it means simply a stupidly imitative culture
with no first hand appreciation of beauty and
dignity and the finer things of the spirit; when it
crushes creative ability; when it permits production only on the lower levels of existence. A
standardized culture that means that Bourges and
Rouen and Amiens and Rheims and Meaux all
have cathedrals isn't so bad; or that Amsterdam
and Antwerp and Haarlem and the Hague have
art museums; or that Caen and Rennes and Tou-
louse and Grenoble have universities. A standardization is deadening when it clamps down with
no feeling for that complete humanization of man
in society which Matthew Arnold said was civilization. It is possible for real culture to exist even
in conjunction with bath tubs, telephones and
motor cars. The crucial thing is whether people
are experiencing and expressing a well rounded,
interesting, vigorous life.

The Nelson influence is still persistent and
dominant in the physical appearance of the city.

His conception of beauty in a residence district, as embodied in the development about his own home, was caught and carried forward by an unusual man, J. C. Nichols. So for miles beyond the property he first laid out are winding roads, lined with attractive homes. His interest in trafficways is perpetuated in a steadily developing municipal system. His concern with landscaping on the grand scale is reflected in the work in progress to provide the city's entrance at the Union Station with a worthy setting and in the idea behind the war memorial that rises on the hill beyond. His taste and his artistic sense still live in the newspaper he established which retains the handsome typography he chose, the literary flavor he gave it, his ideas of good breeding, and which prints on the cover of its Sunday magazine a reproduction of a famous painting instead of a bathing beauty. Finally his passion to enrich the common life, embodied in the art collection he founded, came to full expression in his will by which eventually his entire estate will pass to the public, the income to be used in perpetuity to provide paintings, sculptures, and other art works for the community.

In these respects the life of Kansas City has been lastingly affected by Nelson. So far it has a flavor of its own. But civilization is many sided. In some ways the showing is not so good. If the city's balance sheet were made up it would be something like this:

Industry and material comforts. Great. The

Chamber of Commerce will be glad to furnish statistics on bank clearings, hog receipts, and wheat shipments. Home of the one room apartment with four room efficiency. A daisy. Roll up one wall, a kitchen; pull it down, a living room; clear off the library table, a dining room; manipulate a handle, a bed room.

Literature. Little doing in spite of the gallant efforts of the Quill Club. Eugene Field wrote some of his verse for the old Times and 'then moved on. Alfred Henry Lewis wrote numerous Wolfville stories for The Star and then went to New York. William Allen White as a youngster worked for The Star but retired to Emporia to sprout his fame.

Music. The usual concerts, conservatories, and a Danish composer, Carl Busch. Ed Howe once said of Atchison that for fifty years every girl in town had practiced on the piano until she had driven the neighbors crazy, but Atchison had not produced a single musician. Broadly speaking his remark applies to Kansas City.

Education. Excellent school plant culminating in a junior college. The cultural atmosphere that might be furnished by a college of the liberal arts is missing.

Religion. Highly organized on an efficiency basis. Largest men's Bible class in the country, with elaborate and detailed machinery for maintaining it; a wonder. In theology, overwhelmingly fundamentalist. Out of more than two hundred clergymen twelve or fifteen have organized a Modernist Club and meet occasionally—in secret.

Politics. A formal government, usually commonplace or worse; an informal government of a few powerful interests. When these interests agree in really wanting something they can get it. Ordinarily they are not in agreement and the collective life marks time. A contribution the city has made in the field of municipal government is the combination of agencies usually independent into a comprehensive department of public welfare, with a municipal farm reformatory for the city's prisoners, a loan agency in competition with the loan sharks, and a free legal aid bureau to which the victims of minor injustices may appeal. This contribution was worked out by two one hundred per cent Americans, William Volker, a constructive philanthropist born in Germany, and Jacob Billikopf, a social worker, born in Russia.

Architecture. A punk business district, with a few distinguished buildings and two or three excellent churches. An unusual residential district, already referred to, starting with the Nelson Rockhill development and widely extended. Spanish architecture often used without seeming exotic—except where obviously misplaced and eccentric—because of the traditional and the existing physical connections with New Mexico.

Art. Largely for the future, but assured by endowment. An art institute has several hundred pupils. In addition to the Nelson bequest for the purchase of art works Mrs. Nelson left her estate toward an art museum. With other legacies a fund of nearly two million dollars is already provided for to be used in constructing the necessary galleries. When the Nelson endowment is available Kansas City will have one of the important art foundations of the country.

If we consider both sides of the ledger there are places where the balance goes deeply into the red. Undoubtedly Kansas City, like other cities, has devised a remarkably efficient machine for turning out the material basis for civilization, not by the yard, but by the mile. In America it is usually assumed that when this basis is ready the mechanism will be readjusted to a spiritual product. But the machine has acquired such terrific momentum, it has so thoroughly absorbed the energies of the entire population, it has created so dazzling an ideal of physical comfort measured by money as the real end and object of life, that at times it seems doubtful whether it ever can be stopped long enough to be readjusted. There is a chance that it may simply continue to grind out the same material comforts to the exclusion of the culture and the appreciation of beauty that make the comforts worth while.

So we get back to our original proposition that the civilization of the go-getter tempered by houn' dawg is still in combat with the civilization of beauty where the elbow of the ice sheet protruded and the Missouri made its Great Bend to the east. Sometimes one gets the upper hand, sometimes the other. The marks of the conflict, of the ebb and flow of battle, are everywhere.

Kansas City has created a fine boulevard system. But it has allowed commercial interests to junk long stretches of it with filling stations and billboards. It has put up, or the railroads for it, a monumental Union Station. There is nothing in Europe to equal it. But it permitted the station to stand for years facing a clay bank and it has stood by while the station plaza was flanked with shacks. It has erected a striking shaft for its war memorial on a commanding site. But it has permitted greedy property owners to crowd about with cheap and ugly buildings. It has its miles of winding roads with their attractive homes; if there are comparable residence districts in Europe I have not seen them. But if culture be given Arnold's broad definition as the capacity for criticizing life, these districts as yet have organized a cultural society only in spots. It has made elaborate provision for its unfortunate and has financed many hospitals including one for children that cares for patients from every part of the Middle West. But it has set up a monument for a saloon keeper boss and none for the overshadowing genius who left his great estate to the community. Its public libraries have an unusual circulation of serious books. But its down town organizations for their weekly luncheons frown on high brow stuff and call for pep talks by live wires.

The city expresses a practical religion in generous contributions to humanitarian movements,

and humanitarianism is a factor in civilization.
But a leading clergyman who suggests that one
may doubt the virgin birth and still be a Christian, is frightened by a Fundamentalist outburst
into pleading the next Sunday that he was mis-
quoted; and of one hundred and fifty church
notices printed on a Saturday in The Star, one
third are of eccentric sects. It has built some
stunning viaducts, but has allowed the main entrance to its shopping district to be made a billboard alley. There are stirrings of musical appreciation in its public schools, of musical compo-
sition in its conservatories, of painting in the art
institute. Indeed, it may fairly be said that these
interests are increasingly vigorous and wide
spread. But the overwhelming popular desire for
music over the radio is jazz and there has been
no addition to the Nelson collection of paintings.
A genuine flair for dramatic production has developed in recent years, and some young artists and
actors are painting their own scenery and putting
on their own plays. But there has been an even
greater development of moronic burlesque houses.

The two civilizations are still contending. As
William James said of the universe, it feels like
a real fight. There is no certainty of a favorable
outcome. The issue is in doubt. The city at the
Great Bend, realizing its achievements and sensing its energy, is boundlessly hopeful. So am I.
There is substantial ground for hope. But at
times—I wonder.

SAN ANTONIO:

THE UNSAINTED ANTHONY
By
Dora Neill Raymond

SAN ANTONIO

THE wall that guarded San Fernando has come to dust. The mission outpost of the Spanish Franciscans has expanded into the City of San Antonio, advertised by railway folders as easy of access. Do not believe them. The City, too, has walls.

There are some who think to enter via train, taxi, and registration at a "good hotel." They do not knock at the city gates and there is nothing opened unto them. If they pay appropriately they may experience in San Antonio the same creature comforts that a hundred other cities have to offer. They will find, it is probable, a fair share of the three-hundred-and-sixty-five sunshiny days which, by boast of the Chamber of Commerce, make golfing possible throughout the year. They will make dutiful excursions to the Alamo and Missions, and depart in the same philistine manner in which they came. "San 'Tone," they will call the city they have left. Tourist femina will remember it as the place where she solved that cross-word puzzle Cousin May Etta had tucked into her hand bag. Tourist homo will remember it, perhaps, for a pleasant round of golf at the municipal links or a successful morning's fishing at Medina Lake.

To these good people the city has very definitely been "not at home." The years have brought many such strangers to her gates. Worse far, she has had to suffer from the permanent residence of many of these people, withstand their efforts, constant and disconcerting, to make her over to their proper liking. They would divest her of her mantilla, bob her hair, cap her with a cloche, give her gum to chew and a jazz tune to chew it by. It is no wonder that the City has become most adept in the art of withdrawal, that she has learned subtlety, is reticent, secretive, more prone to brood on memories of the past than smilingly to extend her hands in welcome to the present.

But let no one mistake her seeming impassivity. She is not quiescent. She will not suffer her dignity and her traditions to be impinged upon. Let no one think that she will yield to-day, nor yet to-morrow, her gift of magic, her feeling for romance. Nor does she mean quite to obliterate that strain of gay diablerie to which she owes no small part of her fascination. She may don the garments of right living and wear them with a fine pretence of sober virtue. But that is only because she had found the reward of such behavior to be vastly agreeable—a revived appreciation, a fresher joy in the gipsy tatterdemalia of her vice.

This much conceded, one need not despair of knowing such a city. It is not the hauteur of wealth, the dignity of age—most surely not the aloofness of virtue—that rings her round as unapproachable. One has only to know how to play as well as to work, how to dream as well as to act, and the City will not beckon, it will embrace. She had at first merely stifled a yawn, not lifted her eyebrows. Ah, but if you know how to amuse, how to appreciate, smiles the City, the matter is vastly different. There was an Irishman who learned to turn the trick. For half a century one Bryan Callaghan held firm the city's favor. For a good part of that time, as mayor, he was a near approach to those Wild Geese of Ireland, who lorded it in South America and in the Latin cities of the Continent. Only a few of what was known as the better class of the Americans approved of him. It is probable he approved of them even less. Certainly he must have had a contempt for their misunderstanding of the City. Do but learn his method. A word of wooing Spanish, the leisure to enjoy, courtly phrase or impudent blarney, give these and you may take your pleasure. Such tales you will hear, such delights you will enter into as will mark you, to mutual contentment, as the City's own.

For the City is very like an aged coquette—all eager to display her wares so soon as she is sure you will appreciate. But always, like this old coquette, she will keep something from you. Swift in change, constant in paradox, she will defy even a pledged lover's effort to describe her. Once she was visited by a poet whose vision had been clarified by the suffering of a slow disease, by skill in music and long use of artful words. Even this man failed in his metaphor. "If peculiarities were quills," wrote Sidney Lanier, "San Antonio would be a rare porcupine." This is not apt, for it suggests discomfort, aggressiveness and rigorous uprightness. San Antonio, in spite of its heroic history, has been in each of its two hundred and ten years a city of repose.

That this has been is due, in part, to its geography. The winding river that gives the City its name, gives it, also, its character. Always it approaches, withdraws from the City's heart, says farewell, and then returns to say farewell again. There must be bridges, and yet more bridges, that business may be carried on in the midst of such inappropriate dalliance. And the clipped staccato sounds of to-day in San Antonio must submit to a softening because of the murmurous, languid river. Two men meet, give a brisk handshake, walk forward, make the air tense for a minute with their business jargon. A bridge is to be crossed. One points below to the "sea walls" that were built soon after Galveston's disaster. They stop to argue over whether or not the embankments serve or deride their purpose. A Mexican boy swims by with lazy strokes that scarce disturb the milky greenness of the water. But the flecks of white foam near his sunbronzed body suggest, somehow, the wish to go to Degen's. Perhaps because when a thought is close to the surface almost anything will bring it into consciousness. The men repair to Degen's.

Herr Degen is an aged German with something

more than the Rhineland's classic *Gemütlichkeit* to
commend him; to wit, his own recipe for lager
beer. He has long served those customers whom
he pleased, at what hours he pleased; and if, to-
day, he obeys the federal law and serves no one
at all, he no longer upholds the tradition of San
Antonio's individualism. It is a matter that could
be easily decided by determining the amount of
sidewalk traffic on the two blocks between his
home and the old Menger Hotel. The place was
—is?—not a saloon. There was no bar. The
beer was served, not in steins, but in long glasses.
One could walk to the rear and look out upon the
old man and his assistants at work in the small
brewery, the brewery whose product won first
prize at the St. Louis Exposition, to the wonder
of certain competitors from Milwaukee.

There was another German, one of the modern
city's builders, Father Mahncke, whose palm
garden, in days gone by, provided like diversion.
Before six none but men entered, but at night
they returned, with wives and children, to order
Kalter Aufschnitt and more beer. For the German custom of family stein rights was early
adopted by the Americans. But Father
Mahncke's greatest usefulness was in developing
the City's parks. And none can surely say
whether he beautified these in order to create a
proper suburban atmosphere for beer drinking or
whether he encouraged the granting of concessions
so that a mild imbibing might intensify the appreciation of nature's harmonies.

These Germans, who have grown into the City's life, came over, many of them, because of political troubles in their own country. The Liberal exiles of the forties were of finer mettle than the utilitarian emigrants that followed. In San Antonio, they lost their bitterness and called the street on which they built their homes King William Street, in the belief that the new king might rectify those errors committed by his august brother. But though they gave the street a royal name, they dropped the vons from their own names,—Herff, Kalteyer, Gross, Duerler, Dittmar, Hummel, Meusebach showed their pride only in their honesty and obedience to the laws of their new government. They built a hall for concerts, kept themselves fit by their turnverein— retained the good of the old and gained much good from the new. Their wives carried on the old customs, baked such nut cakes at Christmas as they had baked in Germany, had their windows washed on the accustomed days, whether or not a Texas norther blew or the rains descended in torrents. When the Great War came the name of the street was changed to Pershing Avenue, but the window washing, and cake baking, and the *kaffee klatsches* continued as usual. The street is still a pleasant, shady place, with cooling views of lawns that slope down to the River. Nothing in it chimes with its new name.

One of these Germans who made himself beloved above all others was Dr. Ferdinand Herff. —"The old Doctor," he came to be called to distinguish him from his son, who followed in his footsteps. He did grow to be very old, so old that he could answer only a few of the many who asked his services. But he never changed his fee,—"one dollar"—even though the old figure under the grey shawl his wife had wrapped around him showed fatigue at a call made when younger physicians were sleeping. No wonder that others of his profession were angered! The old Doctor had more skill than any of them. His patients came from other states and the interior of Mexico. A dollar, he would explain, had seemed much money in the old days, and seemed so still. He was consistently negligent in collecting this "much money." It was his wife who, once in so many months, checked up his accounts and sent out his bills. In the afternoon one could see them driving together in leisurely fashion. His grey plaid shawl, her gently Victorian bonnet were pleasant parts of the City's fine mosaic. Someday his letters will be published. They will prove, not only the letters of a pioneer physician, but of a political exile who was constantly and intelligently concerned for the well-being of the Fatherland.

The City's annals tell of an earlier doctor, less skilled but no less picturesque. This other follower of Esculapius lacked the advantage of anatomical study in German universities. Once after an Indian raid, he showed much jubilation over acquiring the body of a very tall Comanche. Next day he exhibited its still pink skeleton. The neighbors were curious as to how he had disposed of those carnal parts that were superfluous. He explained that, quite simply, he had thrown them into the River. Thereupon half the women in town became ill, for the River then supplied the drinking water.

But even such gory cargo as this could not keep the River long in deep disfavor. One cannot but think that the doctor must have been right when he claimed that the old stream had dutifully performed its unaccustomed mission in the night and made itself fresh and clean by breakfast time. It is so hospitable to summer houses, to laughing children who swing out across its purling waters on their grapevine swings, to the pecan trees and the nutting parties that follow its twisting banks that one cannot believe it sinister.

It is true that, in days less civilized, it was hospitable also to the deadly water moccasin. Nurses still tell stories of what has happened to children who ran away to play unguarded near the River. There is a very fascinating Elsie-Venner story of a girl who was veritably charmed by one of these snakes so that she went each day to gaze at it. Finally she brought her little brother that he might look too. Then the snake grew jealous, struck her and she died.

The Mexicans have many legends of the River, for they best understand it. In the hurly-burly of to-day it still speaks their soft language, as it has ever since Don Domingo Ramon made good Spain's claim against the daring young French lordling, St. Denis. It would have been well had

Madame Candelaria been made to talk about this River.

Madame Candelaria was so old that it seemed time had laid a set of lines upon her face to serve the younger women as a pattern for their drawn work. People said she must have been one of those besieged within the Alamo. Madame Candelaria sat in her wrinkles with her ugly *pelon* dog in her lap and did not deny the circumstance. Tourists began to come to see her every day. It was suggested that she charge a fee for their admission. This was done, photographs were sold, she evolved a story and was well paid for its repetition. The *pelon* dog waxed very fat and vicious, and the wrinkles, thankfully, did not diminish. Only the oldest inhabitants remained contemptuous of the history that was being made before their very eyes. But Madame Candelaria could have talked truthfully of the River.

Then the old *tamale* vender, with his odorous burden,—more pungent for the heat that came up through the brazier—he must know the River well. When he pauses on his rounds, it is always on some bridge or other. And on the bridges, too, stand the venders of Mexican candies,—merchants whose stock in trade is borne on a tray strapped to the neck or heaped upon a little folding table. What will you choose, sticky cakes of pecans or brittle, thin ones; sugary rolls, pink or white, with nuts as filling; long streamers of candy, pink or white, also, and very, very sweet, candied bits of pumpkin? One has but to observe the way these old men wave

their gaudy, ribboned "shoo flys" to know at once
that they are River's kin.

In the hotels, now, one can buy these candies
carefully wrapped and boxed with high regard for
cleanliness. But those who passed their childhood
in San Antonio think the *dulces* bought in the sunlight and dust of the street had finer flavor. Then,
too, in dealing thus al fresco, there was the fascination of getting a *pelon*. Has ever a hotel given a
pelon? The pelon is the little something extra—
the *lagniappe* of New Orleans. The Mexican
word comes from the old custom of giving the purchaser something to take home for the baby,—the
bald-headed one, the *pelon*. It is true that some
say the word is a shortening of *peloncillo,* a bit of
candy, but the other explanation is the better. It
affords a valuable commentary on Mexican practice in feeding the young. Even the American
grocers had to observe the custom at one time.
Children asked quite boldly for *pelon* and that place
was taboo that failed to yield it. It is not claimed
that *tamale* venders ever paid this tribute, perhaps
the indulgent Mexicans drew the line at feeding
tamales. to their babies. Then, too, *tamale* merchants do not like to hear this word, *pelon*. Too
often they have been accused of sacrificing a black,
hairless dog or so, the better to plump out the filling of their corn husks.

Perhaps it is because of this omission that the
number of *tamale* venders diminishes so steadily
before the competition of the American managed
restaurants. These are models of efficiency where

one may be served with an entire dinner in which
the only course not seasoned with chile is the after
dinner coffee. Atmosphere, too, is generously included. The walls are hung with Navajo blankets
and Mexican *serapes*. There is abundant pottery
in evidence. Sometimes there is a glimpse on entrance of a wizened crone, half hidden in the shadows, beating maize into a paste on a stone *metate*.
This is for your *tortillas*. Very good these, when
served just after the paste has been mixed with
water and baked on heated iron. But if you try to
eat them cold, you'll think stone has begotten stone,
iron, iron and the corn disappeared, somehow, in
the process. No such delusion ever troubled those
who dined at Madame Garza's. There the *tortillas*
were of an unexcelled perfection.

There was a fascination simply in going to Madame Garza's on Dolorosa Street. It was eminently
respectable. Madame Garza, like Herr Degen,
was an austere artist who made preparations for a
limited number and was discriminating in her cli-
entele. But her restaurant was in her home and
her home bordered on a district of ill repute.
Women of respectability never thought of walking
down its streets alone, for no man wished to be
seen there. It was only with a brother or a father
that one went to Madame Garza's. Then one
walked with eyes straight ahead, though curiosity
would have kept them active. It is true that part
of this district had to be skirted on the way to the
market, but then not on foot. For in San Antonio
no one carries a market basket on the arm, as

women do in other cities. One could gaze at the
Laclede. Windows would be open there. It had
been a favorite hotel for gamblers. Men choose it
still as a fit place for suicide. Past that, the houses
grew secretive. The close shut windows, the almost deserted streets, the hidden aspect of it all,
was disconcerting, made one too restless to think
in proper fashion of fruits, and vegetables, and
family menus.

Close by the market entrance, the Mexican wom-
en crouched above the cages of little singing birds,
gay-colored, helpless. How old these women
looked! Beneath the shadow of their shawls,
peaked out to fend away the sun, their mask-like
faces seemed insensible. And yet a tracery of passion's wrinkles showed they had felt much in vanished youth. They sat with never lifted eyes that
yet appraised their customers, their neighbors'
wares, nay, life itself. They had known all of it,
its different marts, the worth of its merchandise,
the worth of the pay, the worth of death at the
end.

It is well that, in the scheme of things municipal,
a plaza is close by and the cool shadows of San
Fernando's. The plazas are always optimistically
verdant, even in winter time. There are many of
them, and those in the older districts have their
histories. But now, except for the one that spreads
its green before the Alamo, they do not suggest
grim days of war. Even this one can content itself with offering refuge to those who battle in this
age of industry, with warring only against commer-

Market in Military Plaza.

SAN ANTONIO IN THE EIGHTIES

cialism. Here there shall be flowers, it says, and
sunny benches, instead of gainful office buildings.

At night, in the old days, there was music and the
soft rustling of women's dresses, the little moving
lights of cigars and cigarettes, and laughter under
the indulgent stars. Travelers of half a century
ago have written of the bespangled troupe of
mountebanks who used to parade there, drum and
trombone going clamorously before, to gain a crowd
for their evening's performance. Once the *Banda
Policia* of the City of Mexico sealed friendship by
playing its fine best before the Alamo.

Never is the plaza gayer than on the twenty-
first of April, when the city celebrates the victory
of San Jacinto. The flower-decked cars and carriages divide to circle it in opposite directions and
a mock battle, with blossoms for weapons, is waged
before the grey old Alamo. It was a congress-
man's wife, they say, who brought the pretty idea
back from the Riviera. It has taken kindly to
transplanting. This part of the spring carnival is
always a success. Given flowers, pretty girls and
an historic background, it cannot fail to be. Then,
too, the Government, itself, lends aid. From Fort
Sam Houston comes the regimental band, trim
officers, fresh from the Point, complaisant cannon,
their caissons rustling in an unaccustomed garni-
ture of flowers. To be sure, Uncle Sam levies tribute, and to such extent that the City is becoming
known as the mother-in-law of the Army. Its
daughters make the sacrifice not unwillingly and
having linked themselves with the Army seldom

leave it,—although they may indulge themselves
more than once in a change of husbands. San Antonio is a city as honestly proud of her record for
divorce as of her record for matrimony. She
boasts, herself, that she has flourished under seven
flags.

But carnival time is not the time to be taking
thought as to which column of statistics one's ac-
tions may commit one. It comes when spring has
made the night air soft and the heat is still but
gentle. Arches of gay lights fling themselves across
the streets, like the serpentine streamers of the
crowds that pass beneath. Music, torchlights,
Mardi Gras cars—massively grotesque with alle-
gory, girls who queen it for a night, such a court of
royalty as most delights democracy, who could be
serious when the city flashes castanets? At night
on the plazas, *chile*-stands spring up, spread with
red table-cloths, lighted by oil lamps. Old crones,
their sombre shawls draped gracefully, serve steaming dishes, each one more highly seasoned than the
last. Children and *pelon* dogs play beneath the
tables. The children one may step on. The dogs
must be treated with consideration.

At the Queen's Ball there will be satin covered
programmes, orchids and long-stemmed roses from
St. Louis, French frocks and royal jewels sent
from Tiffany's. But the few within, as well as the
crowd without, keep to the spirit of San Antonio.
In New York, during the opera season, there are
many who stand each night on the pavements for
a glimpse of the exquisite ladies who must pass

from their limousines to the entrance. No beauty is
ever cheered, nor expects to be. It is gayer to go to
the Queen's Ball. Some years the court arrives in
carnival cars, a milky way in motion down the winding streets. The crowd masses thick about them.
Torch lights glimmer on upturned faces, pricked
out, star fashion, in the dusk. Those of the court
who arrive first cluster at the windows to watch the
approach of the others. It takes grace and poise
to descend from a carnival car when all the world
is looking. One princess of the night, in doing so,
has left a pleasant memory. Those in the windows
knew she had refused a Mardi Gras queendom out
of loyalty to her own city. They called her name
and cheered when the lumbering car that bore her
paused and the ladder was placed against its towering grotesquerie. The princess stood a moment
in silhouette against the night, then raised both
hands to throw a kiss up to the windows. Her cape
fell from her and, quite spontaneously, a cry of admiration for her beauty came from those below.
One man, an uncouth fellow from the Lord knows
where, reached out his hand to help in her descent.
With military quickness, an officer from the Post
pushed him back and held his arms to her. But my
lady ignored him, slipped her hand into that of the
unknown cavalier, and descended with as pretty a
grace as any princess in a fairy tale. This was
Julia of the House of Armstrong. Her name
should be recorded.

In April, the wild flowers, too, are holding carnival. They are their gayest on Alamo Heights.

There is a bravura about these vagrant, fragrant denizens of the field that would shock their sisters of the north. Bluebonnets, purple verbena, wine cups, thistle blooms—thorned alarmingly—sturdy nigger toes thrusting themselves above the dainty tracery of queen's lace handkerchief, all clamor pell mell for the favors of the sultan sun. And this they have done each year since the King of Spain set his seal to the deed that placed on Spanish maps, the township San Fernando. The wild flowers know the old boundaries as well as the City's fathers: stone mound at the River's head, stone mound around the live oak tree. More than a hundred years after the City's founding, old men were summoned to court to tell what other old men had told them of the ancient landmarks. The lost deed they had seen, and described so well its contents that a young Canadian engineer was able to survey the township. The Supreme Court of the state sustained the City against those who had encroached on land within its boundaries. Six leagues by these old mounds, the Cibolo on the east, the Leon on the west, the Jacolitos, and, in between, the helter skelter lines of Texas wild flowers. To modern thinking, the boundaries were perplexing. But, in those days, it would have been daring Providence and the Comanches had attempt been made to establish metes and bounds more definite.

Alamo Heights has seen fit, in these later days, to incorporate itself. The wild flowers are no longer to be picked. There is an Irish mayor, the bachelor brother of the Misses O'Grady whose din-

ners are remembered by all of epicurean palate.
If one is to remember San Antonio most pleasantly,
one must dine at the Argyle. Its flavor then will
linger. Army men and their wives have sung the
praises of the sisters O'Grady in every part of the
Union. Kipling's Judy O'Grady is scarce less
famous. Had Judy known how to chill a watermelon to exactly the right temperature, to plug it
and fill it with champagne, as they do at the Argyle, could she have tossed a cake together with the
unerring abandon of the O'Gradys, no man would
have coupled her shining name with that of a mere
Colonel's lady.

Very different from the Argyle, but boasting its
own peculiar gustatory excellence, was a curious
little place in the old City Market House across
from the Library. It was kept by Ernest—
surname unknown. Bare tables, pewter knives
and iron stone china ensured the place from
feminine invasion. The excellence of its steaks and
certain other dishes made it the noontime rendezvous of all the lawyers who were too fortunately
busy to return to their families. It was said that
Ernest had been the head chef of Maximilian. The
story made it easy to understand the peculiarly sad
expression of the Mexican Emperor in that portrait showing him just before execution. Even to
a prospective martyr of St. Peter's faith, Heaven
could promise no glories such as Ernest's steaks.

Another famous dining place was, and happily
still is, the Menger. It was built before the Civil
War. It is said that Robert E. Lee knew it ap-

preciatively. Certainly a goodly number of lesser
celebrities have passed its portals, lingered in its
patio and bought gay boutonnieres from the little
flower-sellers that haunted it at evening. In the old
days it was the favorite meeting place for stockmen. There was always a line of chairs on the sidewalks, in front and on the side, tilted at precarious
angles. The chairs would come down with a bang
of protest against some yarn of more than usual
exaggeration, more quietly when adjournment was
taken to the bar.

Aleck Sweet, of Texas Siftings, has told the
story of the effect of the Menger on a cowboy of
the days when the species was disingenuous. The
cowboy was told by the clerk that dinner was served
from twelve to three. He whooped amazement at
the prospect of such gourmandizing. But at full
meridian he ambled to his table and did not rise till
three, when he announced that he "felt sort o' satisfied and fixed up for business." This last he found
no doubt, in equal measure. There were any number of places that offered opportunities for the con-
tracting of such business as cowboys came to town
for. In San Antonio, virtue has never raged supreme. There was on Military Plaza and West
Commerce Street, the Silver King, a gambling
house conducted most courteously by Arthur Ware.
Mr. Ware was a gentleman who had hospitable concern for the safety and well-being of his customers.
In 1896, Harry Bennett, a noted gambler, was
killed on the stairs by Bob Marks. An instant
later, Mr. Ware administered capital punishment

on Bob Marks. Nothing less than the state law of
1905, making it a felony to conduct a gambling
house and providing for injunction proceedings,
could have put such a place out of business.

On Main Plaza, flaunting itself before the Court
House, was the Crystal. It had three proprietors,
Billy Sims, Sam Berliner and Will Ford. It was
this Billy Sims who was tried for the killing of
Ben Thompson of Austin and of King Fisher. The
two unfortunates were at the exact location where
the Spanish fathers first pitched camp. They were
not there for historical research but to observe from
their box the sprightly performance on the stage of
Jack Harris's Variety Theatre. The homicide
seems to have been planned with the nicety of a
political assassination. Certainly there was con-
certed action and the shots were fired by more than
one. Everyone was satisfied with the result, including the prompt acquittal of Billy Sims. It
seemed fair enough,—Ben Thompson had had his
innings in the place. He had killed Jack Harris
there with a double barreled shot gun. Sims was a
quiet, well-dressed man with manners that would
have been a credit to the gentlemen gamblers of
Bret Harte.

Most desperadoes, strangely enough, are reported
as answering to the conventional description of a
house dog—"gentle, fond of children." Aleck
Sweet used to tell a story of how one of his sons
was nearly killed by the misdirected kindness of
Ben Thompson. Thompson at one time was Chief
of Police of Austin and his little daughter became

a friend of Mr. Sweet's son. One day she asked him to "stay to dinner." He stayed. Ben Thompson sat at the head of the table and when the little boy's plate was empty would fix his eye on him and say, "Have some more steak, sonny. Have some gravy and hot biscuit." That night a very sick little boy moaned that Ben Thompson had made him eat, and eat until he was ready to cry. Next day the too hospitable host met the father and mildly berated him for neglecting sufficiently to feed his offspring.

Before the days of Ben Thompson's fame, an old gambling house on South Flores Street had already added a quota to the picturesque wickedness of San Antonio. This was The Black Elephant, resort of stockmen, buffalo hunters and the old trail men. It got its name from a big slate colored elephant, painted on one of the outside walls. Here Melvin Ferrar gambled. He could afford the pastime. West of the Pecos his cattle roamed over a ranch of ten million acres. He set his stakes at somewhere west of the North Star.

Of equal age was The Buckhorn Saloon, which later degenerated into a sort of museum of horns, hides and snakeskins. It was here that there occurred the tragedy of the parrot. From 1850 on, the Butterworth Stage Road stretched its sandy, sinuous way for two thousand miles from San Francisco to the Buckhorn. Up to this time, religious processions in the town were very common. The last sacrament was borne through the streets to the dying, while surpliced priests attended it

with pious chanting. *"Ora pro nobis,"* they intoned.
And the parrot swung in his hoop and intoned,
"Ora pro nobis," also. After the bird took up its
residence at the Buckhorn, it used to send its prayers after the departing stage coach. In view of the
frequent Indian scalping parties, they were appropriate.

The parrot was kept because the saloon keeper
thought the *"ora pro nobis"* had a salutary influence on the keno and poker games. Men felt that
they were in the shadow of the sanctuary, if not of
death itself. Honesty seemed the better policy.
Later, the bird became corrupted and mixed foul
oaths with its churchly chanting. Then he was
shot by a gentle desperado, who could not sanction
sacrilege.

Just where sacrilege begins, of course, is a very
fine point on which one cannot expect Methodists,
mystics and desperadoes to be in full agreement.
The Roman Catholics, alone of Christians, are capable of mixing the affairs of God and man with
profit and satisfaction. Take the matter of naming the River. The Indians called it Chem-quem-
ka-ko, "Old-man-coming-home-from-the-lodge," because it meanders seven miles between its springs
and the City, whereas a sober river could get over
the ground in about three. The Spaniards mistook
this descriptive name for that of some tribal god,
so they piously renamed the stream in honor of St.
Anthony. Thereupon the natives, believing their
new friends had translated the name as best they
could, concluded Saint Anthony to be a very jovial

saint. They accepted him, forthwith into their calendar. Very willingly, the Spaniards preserved the illusion and St. Anthony took his place in strange disguise above the altar of the old Cathedral. He appeared in this early mural, astride a mustang and in the war paint of a bold Comanche,—halo floating above and a buffalo scuttling before to escape his winging arrow. It came to be the custom for the Spaniards and their converts to do honor to the Saint's day by riding through the streets at full tilt, in pious emulation of the metamorphosed Paduan.

One can imagine that Captain Jack Hays was most contemptuous of the new St. Anthony and his halo. Captain Hays was one of those Indian fighters whose intimate knowledge of the different tribes led him to believe the only good Indian was a dead one. In command of the Rangers, stationed in the City before the Civil War, he much deprecated adding to the deviltry of the place any such celebrations as the Hispano-Indian saint evoked on his name day. Not, of course, that the Rangers were not sociable and fond, themselves, of celebrations. When the Indians came in with deer and buffalo hides to buy a big time, they were not disturbed in their purchase unless their exuberance became unduly dangerous. Then the party was quickly eliminated from the landscape.

The City, whenever possible, has encouraged sociability. That is why retired stockmen and army officers make the place the home of their old age. That is why it is a favorite refuge for the political

exiles of neighboring Mexico. The City has a hospitable come-hither-air for those who seek it out for
purposes not utilitarian. She offers, if you wish it,
"a free and lazy, loloppy sort of life," and tolerant
indifference of conspiracy. But for those who come
as the missionaries of commercial uplift, she has no
welcome. They may go to Dallas and assist in the
erection of a city on the 1930 model. Losoya, Sole-
dad, Navarro, Flores, Dolorosa, these are not
proper street names for the addresses of skyscrapers. They were bequeathed to the city by the Spanish families who came from the Canaries. The Ver-
amendi House, the old Twohig place, the Ursuline
Convent, plead that their philosophy of life may
still be cherished.

A very modern department store advertises itself as in the heart of San Antonio. Prospective
grooms from Mexico come there, appropriately, to
buy the trousseaus for their fiancées. Perhaps, geo-
graphically, it is in the City's centre. But the true
heart of San Antonio is the Alamo, fronted by a
quiet plaza and flanked by the drowsy, comfortable
Menger. Some slight attempt, it is true, has been
made to introduce business even into the citadel.
There is a counter at the entrance where post cards
and pamphlets can be bought. But sales are made
most unobtrusively. The shades of·the men who
gave their lives there—men of sword, and bowie
knife and gun, knew much of the starry heavens
and the prairies, but nothing at all of ledgers.

Even the most modern of the City's merchants
has had to bow to the local tolerance of beggary.

The only concession made is that, whereas the profession of the unprofessional was once exercised at all times, it is now arranged that beggars, once a week, shall come for their dole direct to the business office, without molesting customers. This invasion of efficiency is a great handicap on the beggars. It robs them of all chance of developing technique. The artist in individualism now makes his living otherwise.

There was Philip, or Felipe, who regularly carried on negotiations with the best business houses in San Antonio, and with no more expense to himself than begging would involve. His stock was a bundle of yellowed papers. These he wrapped carefully and delivered at stated intervals to regular customers. May St. Peter note that he was never turned off empty handed. He worked from dawn to dusk, did no one harm, and his activities were quite as serviceable as those of many other citizens. Another odd character, a former slave, whose exquisite manners must have mirrored those of his master, evolved a costume of such mingled pathos and absurdity, that money was freely given him out of pity and as payment for amusement. His old black broad-cloth suit was extended to outlandish size by wires and paper padding, and yet worn with such unapproachable dignity that even children feared to laugh at him.

The City understands these gentle zanies. It understood, too, young Sam Maverick. Son of the Sam Maverick who was one of San Antonio's early heroes, he undertook to guide the destiny of the

Maverick Bank. Its failure hurt a very goodly number of the population. No one questioned the unfortunate president's honesty, no one censured him. He gave everything that he had in atonement for his ignorance of business. Men seldom speak of his misfortune. They praise him as one of the bravest of the Terry Rangers and one of the organizers of the famous Belknap Rifles, the City's own. This crack squad, for fifteen or twenty years, was more the favorite with the fair than any company at the Post.

Recently there died in San Antonio, a New Englander who long had made his home there and had increased his wealth to large proportions. He has left his estate to be used as a retreat for "elderly women of culture without means,"—a bequest in itself a gentle recognition of the City's influence. Men say of him now that "while in a sense a foreigner and never quite naturalized, he was high grade."

There was a time, a horrible time to remember, when the City became commercialized. That was when the Government plopped down upon it one of the largest of the wartime concentration camps. San Antonio never will quite forgive this, nor, perhaps, will the men who were sent there. It brought to the surface in malignant form all of the evil tendencies that peace had kept in dark abeyance.

The old Post had seemed no more than a suburb of the City itself. Its clock tower, its trim parade grounds, the shady lawns and hospitable homes of the officers did not suggest the shameless waste and

hurry, the mechanic thoroughness and devastation
that is war.

Within the City, closely nestled on the River, is
the Arsenal. It is doubtful whether the children
who were its neighbors knew just what an arsenal
was for. It seemed so innocently pleasant a part of
the landscape. There was a mound or two of cannon balls on the lawn, with some old fashioned cannon. They seemed as void of harm as the weapons
that visitors stared at in the Alamo.

The officers had pleasant wives, were in search of
maids for wives, or frankly ready for flirtation.
The children from the Upper and Lower Post rat-
tled to school each morning in the Government am-
bulance. The Army seemed an aggregate of more
or less happy families who had elected to spend
their time in San Antonio. A new Post was being
built that promised to become as pleasant as the
old ones.

In 1898, the City had known, for a time, a khaki
army. There had been excitement over the barbarities that Spain was practicing on Cuba. This, the
City understood. Spanish cruelty was, perhaps,
like that of Santa Anna's men. "Remember the
Maine," she adjudged as similar to, but not quite
so inciting, as the older cry of "Remember the
Alamo." She watched her men enlist with appropriate enthusiasm. On the grounds where every
year an International Fair was held (international
because Mexico joined hands across the border), a
heartily energetic gentleman from New York was
organizing the Rough Riders. It was a little diffi-

cult to become accustomed to a Rough Rider who wore eye-glasses. None of the bowlegged cow punchers, who before had helped to make the City's history had ridden thus accoutred. But the gentleman showed himself no tenderfoot. He was granted a choice assortment of her sons. Also Captain McAdoo let down the bars of admission to the Belknap Rifles. The personality of Judge Robert B. Green was such that the recruits he gathered for his former company were impressed with the honor of their new connection. Other companies were formed. Some of the men were sent to Cuba and brought back glory, and some were only sent to Florida and a diet of embalmed beef. But the affair was shortly over. War time titles were dropped. Captain McAdoo returned, but died soon after,—one of those victims of war to whom it is not granted to die in battle. The rough riding gentleman from New York continued to cavort spectacularly, and sometimes to good purpose, but only athwart the field of politics. Fort Sam Houston dreamed and danced, paraded, flirted.

In April of 1917, it was jolted into more martial action. The City that, long ago, had been chosen as the base for the frontier army at El Paso was selected as a base for the gathering and training of men to be sent overseas. Row upon row of ugly frame buildings sprang up. Men poured into them from the east, south, north and west. And the sins of the City went out to welcome them. Some wives came, worried and unhappy, or else feverishly gay.

But in the training camps there could be no place
for women.   Men were made into officers on the
field.   Lieutenants, captains, were college men, who
a few months before knew less of drill than foot-
ball or fraternity affairs.   On Saturday night, the
privates swarmed into the City.   No force of State
Rangers could have kept them in order, had they
shown themselves unruly.   But for the most part,
they were pitifully obedient, ready to do as they
were ordered, ready to believe as they were ordered,
willing to die when that was ordered.   Professors
of history, patriotically deputed by the State University, came to teach them quite all that they
should know.

The ladies of the City sent their cars to give the
sick men outings.   Privates were invited into homes
that now they cannot enter,—and, perhaps, would
not wish to.   They were danced with and fêted in a
gorgeous orgy of democracy.   Close to the Alamo,
a fine old home was turned into a place of amusement by the indefatigable "Y."   Matches were
made, marriages hastened to ensure a proper quota
for the generation that was to enjoy a world safe
for democracy.   Among the citizens there were endless drives,—drives for money, drives for men.
Merchants gave freely.   They could well afford to.
Their sales had doubled.   All too often, their prices
doubled also.   No male clerk was safe from inquiry
as to why he was not in uniform.   Everyone must
go.   Their positions would be held open for their
return.   "Minute Men" spoke on the Liberty Loans
at the theatres.   Canada's slogan was thrown out

for the City's emulation. "Give until it hurts. Then keep on giving."

Canny business men learned that they could make a tidy bit by using the swill from the camps to fatten porkers. On the streets they joked each other on the profits of their "hog ranches." And the women sewed and made bandages or showed patriotic fervor by the multiplicity and democracy of their wartime entertainments. But the dress of the Red Cross no more means purity than an evening gown may mean abandon. War, when it brings suffering, perhaps may purify but the preparation for war gives, surely, the same heightened opportunity for evil that it does for good. If the worst gossip of the city proved as nimble with her fingers as her tongue, her piles of bandages won her forgiveness.

Only one form of criticism was taboo. Of the war, of the Army, of the Government, nothing but good should be said. When the son of one of the leading lawyers of the City lost control of his plane and crashed to his death, there were hushed whispers that through some oversight, some loss of medical certificates, he had been inoculated three times instead of once, that he had been in no condition to go up. The Government named one of the flying fields for him. The City became pleasantly proud of her young hero. Only a few remained curious as to the manner of his death. Their curiosity, of course, was out of season. Nor was it patriotic to question the expediency of some of the entertainments countenanced by the officers, to inquire as to the prevalence of certain diseases, the causes of epidemics. San Antonio, cosmopolitan, leisurely, picturesquely wicked San Antonio, had become one hundred per cent American. The United States Army had tilted an infantry hat at rakish angle on the City's head, and called her, between a hiccough and a shout, "San 'Tone." She deserved it.

How far away seemed then the Mission days, how impotent the River! And yet it was these ruined Missions, this murmurous River, things inanimate, that kept secure the spirit of their being,—waited until there would again be time to soothe and to engender dreams. Swift and smooth shining, the stream meandered on, as in the old days when it charmed the poet, Lanier. There were, as then, vistas of sweet lawns to be seen from the bridges, willows bending low to lave their branches, trailing Spanish moss to touch its surface. The River still combed the sea green tresses of the wandering water grass. Its muted lisping still floated up among the noise of traffic, like some dove voiced Spanish nun, praying heaven's mitigation of all battles of trade or arms. And in the early twilight, dreams still came whispering adown the current among the willow sprays.

Year after year, the Mexicans have performed *Los Pastores* on the *Fiesta de Santos Reyes*. The old miracle play was enacted at Christmas time, as always. Its lesson,—a glorification of creation; its blessing of peace on earth to men of good will, after so many repetitions, unlearned and unappreciated.

Without the City's boundaries, past disused *ace-quias,* rising above the low *mesquite,* the twin towers of Concepción, the exquisite window of San José, Missions Espada and San Juan, still offered the sermons of their crumbling stones. Soldier, priest, artist, patient Indian convert, whose work will best endure? All of them are the City's fathers,—men of the frontier, leaving old worlds, old ideas, to master those that promise better things, and trailing still, as fetters, the faults and obsessions that have made a heavy past.

As it was with them, so it is with the City's children. Something of the spirit of the old place has entered into them, penetrated to the marrow, or, as the Spaniards better phrase it, *'hasta sus entrañas,"* and must remain till death disintegrates their carnal being. How far can they go forward? What goal can the City reach? *"Pues, quién sabe?"* murmurs the old River. "The way is not always forward. It is well to go slowly. Life is good."

LOS ANGELES:

BALLYHOOERS IN HEAVEN
By
Paul Jordan-Smith

"You cannot speak to us,
   O George Washington,
But you can speak to God:
Tell Him to make us good American citizens."

(Inscription on the wing of a great bronze American eagle in the foyer of Grauman's Metropolitan Theatre, illustrating the unconquerable faith of the modern Angeleno.)

LOS ANGELES

THE Pueblo del Rio de Nuestra Señora La Reina de Los Angeles de Porciuncula, known to winter pilgrims as Los Angeles, and to the local inhabitants as Los, is, in reality, less a city of angels than a paradise of realtors and a refuge for the rheumatic. It bears, however, a much worse name, in the literary journals of this country, than it deserves. San Francisco, its bitter rival, receives to this day the polite huzzas of the elect, who are yet misled by a fiction. For the New Yorker, reading his history of American letters, is convinced that the northern city is still the Bohemian, pagan, intellectual metropolis of the far West. He is apparently unaware that the earthquake and prohibition have transformed the town of Mark Twain and Bret Harte into a fair likeness of Kansas City and Peoria. Such is the vitality of tradition. For Los Angeles the same gentleman reserves the epithet,—"The soul of Iowa."

Perhaps the fault lies in the ironic power of a name, for, if its history is to be credited, the place has never been angelic. For almost 100 years after its founding in 1781, it was a town of rough and ready, draw-yer-gun-and-be-damned-to-yuh westerners, as independent in their ways and as true in their aims as the gold-seeking gentry who made San Francisco famous.

From the city of narrow, motor-crowded streets, anaemic mid-westerners, and sappy "metaphysicians" back to the days when swarthy dons stalked about the *Plaza* in tight green jackets trimmed with gold; when the caballeros came thundering by, gleaming with silver; when cafeterias were gay drinking places, and when a mild city ordinance suggested that white men should avoid consummating their amours with Indian lasses in the public streets, is a far off shout. Yet once upon a time this Mecca of the middle classes was dominated by such gentlemen as Nasario Dominguez, Bernardo Yorba, José Sepulveda and Don José María Verdugo, who, in their picturesque serapes and wide sombreros, made this southern town a place of vivid distinction. Early of a spring morning one might see the haughty Don Antonio María Lugo come prancing by on his jet black steed, followed by a mounted procession of sixteen sons, all well over six feet in height and arrayed, each of them, in finery that exceeded by far the value of a modern flivver.

Gone are the favorite sports of the Latin civilization that enlivened this southern Pacific coast. Once men shouted at bull fights, within a stone's throw of the Plaza; once the streets were strewn with the carcasses of heroic cocks; once the gay balls and fandangoes and feasts lasted for half a week; once the streets resounded till midnight with the laughter of tipsy revellers and the playful shots

LOS ANGELES IN THE LATE FIFTIES

of care-free worshippers of Chance. Now all, all is still save the rattle of Fords and the clatter of thick plates in the steaming cafeterias.

Once the populace of Nigger Alley so resented convention that when Henry Allen in deed and truth did lawfully take and marry Doña Concha it vented its righteous indignation, celebrated its disgrace by mobbing the hapless bridegroom with old eggs and empty bottles. Now it brays with the Rotarians and joins the Eastern Star.

Once the hills were clad with vines and the presses were hard put in the service of parched throats; once the lights were never dimmed in the Bella Union, and the El Dorado flowed with golden liquors. Now the Bella Union is no more and the El Dorado long ago bore a steeple and was transformed into a Methodist chapel by Parson Bland. All is deadly, dumb and democratic.

But these later consummations were a long and a furious time coming.

In 1854, with a population of less than four thousand, Los Angeles "averaged one homicide a day for every day in the year." * According to the same authority "The Southern Californian of March 7, 1855, carried this brief notice: 'Last Sunday night was a brisk night for killing. Four men were shot and killed and several wounded in a shooting affray,' "

The Los Angeles Star expressed its dismay concerning an unpleasantness in these words: "Men hack one another in pieces with pistols and other

* A History of California, by Robert Glass Cleland.

cutlery as if God's image were of no more worth
than the life of one of the two or three thousand
dogs that prowl about our streets."

In 1853 there were more murders in California
than in any state of the Union, and Los Angeles
proudly led the rest of California by a large majority. It may well be noted just here that Los Angeles had been the metropolis of the state for a
period of sixty-five years during the pioneer epoch:
San Francisco came into sudden prominence at the
time of the gold rush of 1849.

At about the same period, according to Mr. Harris Newmark,* there occurred a happy incident
which is typical of the frontier milieu and its code
of justice: A certain man "presented himself as
candidate for the office of sheriff; and, in order to
capture the vote of the native element, he also offered to marry the daughter of an influential Mexican. A bargain was concluded and, as a result, he
forthwith assumed the responsibilities and dangers
of both shrieval and matrimonial life.

"Before the sheriff had possessed this double
dignity very long, however, a gang of horse-thieves
began depredations around Los Angeles. A posse
was immediately organized to pursue the desperadoes, and after a short chase they located the band
and brought them in. . . . Imagine the sheriff's
dismay when he found that the leader was none
other than his own brother-in-law whom he had
never before seen!

"To make the story short, the case was tried and

* Sixty Years in Southern California, by Harris Newmark.

the prisoner was found guilty; but owing to influence (to which most juries in those days were very
susceptible) there was an appeal for judicial leni-
ency. Judge Dryden, therefore, in announcing the
verdict, said to the sheriff's brother-in-law,—'The
jury finds you guilty as charged . . . but the jury
recommends clemency. Accordingly, I declare you
a free man, and you may go about your business.'
Thereupon someone in the courtroom asked: 'What
is his business?' To which the Judge, never flinch-
ing, shouted: 'Horse-stealing, sir! horse-stealing!'"

From 1848 to 1854 there was only one prominent
negro in this lively city, Peter Biggs, famous as
the "Black Democrat" and the municipal barber.
On the side Pete was go-between for lonely gentlemen and ladies of easy virtue. Moreover he was
a speculator. In the year 1849, according to Major
Horace Bell, San Francisco was infested with enormous rats. Los Angeles, on the other hand, bristled
with cats. The negro, having an eye to American
business efficiency, undertook a monopoly of
southern rat catchers for the northern city. Fur-
tively he walked the streets at night and while the
white and Mexican populations were busied in
shooting, cutting, gambling, drinking and making
unlovely love, he experienced but little difficulty in
gathering cats. These were caged, crated and
shipped to San Francisco, where they fetched in
open market from sixteen to one hundred dollars
apiece.

A few years later the same gentleman had an

unfortunate experience as a result of social prejudice. One of the characteristically democratic
"grand balls" of the period was being given, and
the belle of the room was a particularly popular
prostitute, known familiarly as Doña Ramona.

Hither came one of the city's elect citizens, Mr.
Aleck Bell, seeking amusement and the lady's hand
for the opening waltz. Doña Ramona informed
the gentleman that she was engaged for the moment, but would be pleased to grant him the second dance. But when the music began Bell was
enraged to behold the damsel in the arms of none
other than black Pete, now resplendent in correct
evening dress, and radiating pleasure, pride and
perfume.

There was only one thing for a gentleman to do,
draw his gun and have an immediate understanding. The music was stopped by the flourish of a
Colt, and in icy tones the Southern gentleman inquired whether Madame preferred a nigger to a
white man.

"Sir," she said, "I consider it a privilege."

In reply to this social heresy Mr. Bell opened
fire, and the negro, with flying coat-tails, fled from
the room, nor did he stop until he reached the harbor of San Pedro, twenty miles away. To show
the generous and forgiving nature of these warm
blooded people, however, it is necessary to relate
that next day the whole town grieved for its enterprising barber, Aleck Bell repented of his little im-
petuosity and the negro was received to the bosom
of the metropolis once more.

One must, in fairness, say this much: The early American pioneers were not responsible for the present state of things.

They were upstanding, fearless men who, seeing the tremendous opportunities that were here in the Fifties, and sensing a larger freedom than prevailed in New England, came to this spot to raise sheep, cattle and oranges for the good of their own souls and the greater advantage of their families. They dwelt in large, thick-walled, wide-doored comfortable quarters, and exercised a generous hospitality; and, within the limits of decency, were men of their own opinions. They did not stampede nor snivel. Most of their descendants have shriveled down to dull conformity, or gone to the devil from too great a prosperity.

The stranger, however, will find at least this remnant of the ancient ways: a normal and wholesome lack of suspicion. The Westerner going East finds that his Traveller's check is more often than not suspected of being counterfeit, and at the bank to which he has been directed he will be treated as a possible thief. Here the Easterner is astounded to find his practically unidentified check accepted with careless ease, his good standing assumed, and his person uninsulted. His only devil is the realtor.

It is more than possible that the downfall of Los Angeles came about through the following sequence of events: The years 1863-64 were the rainless years, and during the severe and unexpected drought cattle perished by the thousands. The ranchers were desperate: many were utterly ru-

ined. One ranch of 27,000 acres was offered for
the price of taxes—one hundred and fifty dollars
—, and city lots, now worth hundreds of thousands, were refused at a dollar and a half apiece.
Then it was that the ranchers opened great sections of their land to colonists from the Middle
West. At about this time the news had gone
abroad that the now vaunted climate was inimical
to the consumption germ. And then came the railroads. In 1877 the Southern Pacific ran down
from the north, and in the early eighties it was
joined by the Sante Fé. These two railway companies flew at one another's throats in deadly competition. During the rate war that followed, the
price of a ticket from the Mississippi Valley to the
land of health and open spaces fell to the round
sum of one hundred cents. Who could resist? The
diseased poured in and spread their tents upon a
thousand hills. The rheumatics were next, and
they signalled to their neighbors, the retired farmers
from the chilly corn belt. Tuberculars, rheumatics
and retired farmers! A susceptible crew,—easy
pickin's for the Boston mind-healers and preachers
of spiritual uplift. The parasites swarmed in
droves to the feast. Out of this mess there grew
and fattened the livest and most persistent gang of
land pirates that the world has ever known. It became a crime to criticise California; a felony to
whisper of an earthquake; to frown upon the
climate was equivalent to committing rape. The
old timers, filled with nausea, sought their graves.
    Yet even while they still invigorated the earth

with the glamor of their haleness, the suggestion of a certain ill fame in the city's officially angelic title was, as we have seen, already historic. And even this year of grace and puritanism (1925) the same suggestion is frequently noticeable. This is partly owing to the influx of eastern criminals who, because of the inconvenient migration of millionaires from New York and Chicago, and because of the rigors of a severe climate, elect to spend their winters in Southern California: owing also to the alleged immoralities of the moving picture kings and queens: owing, finally, to the grasping nature of the aforementioned realtors, who operate without regard to season.

On the other hand, the ill repute of the city may arise from the disappointment of the expectant tourist who, having read of the above recited delinquencies, hopes to find the place an American Port Said, reeking with wine and the hootcheekootchee. He arrives to discover a population of Iowa farmers and sun-burned old maids in an endless chain of cafeterias, movie palaces and state picnics. He bursts over a whole column of some obscure eastern magazinelet, and declares that the city of the angels is just as dull as the traditional kingdom of heaven.

And he is exactly right; for Los Angeles is a wholly typical, post-Volsteadian, American big town. Its charms are matters of climate and outlying scenery—things that most of our other cities do not have in such abundance. The buildings, streets and people might well be the buildings, streets and people of Dallas, Cleveland or Des Moines.

Apart from the climate and scenery, the sole things that stand out are glittering sedans of European make, owned by ex-farm hands and café wenches who, because of a dimple or a wart, have been enthroned in the gaudy kingdom of the screen. These vacant-eyed children of the back alleys provide thrills for retired Iowans, whilst they themselves seek new sensations in ancient vices imported from the sea ports of the Mediterranean.

Well, what of it? If the place exhibits all the vices of the middle plains, it is also alive with the same eagerness in pursuit of an illusory progress and a conventionally idealized culture. I am convinced that there is much more familiarity with "high brow" books in this too frequently berated city than in any other considerable center of population west of Chicago. Marcel Proust, James Joyce, Paul Morand, Rémy de Gourmont and Jacob Wasserman are pawed over in a hundred women's clubs every week, and the shelves of the average middle-class home are laden with the novels of Sheila Kaye-Smith, Brett Young, D. H. Lawrence, and Joseph Hergesheimer; the walls are hung with Austin Spares, and copies of Gauguin and Matisse; the pianos are scattered over with the dotted sheets of Strauss, Debussy, Palmgren and Rimsky Korsakoff.

The people who thus decorate themselves may have no genuine culture; may, indeed, be addicted to the secret use of chewing gum, and be furtive admirers of Mary Pickford: but these are national crimes and are not to be attributed to a local weakness. I repeat, therefore, that the citizens of Los Angeles may have the vices of the Middle West, but they also have its redeeming virtue—a fevered yearning for vaster mental horizons.

Tame? Certainly. The people who daily flivver from Hill Street to Hollywood do the goose step to perfect time. They will stand for anything, vote for anything, believe anything that appears in public print. They will permit themselves to live under more nonsensical ordinances than any people on earth. A suburban example of this mania may be cited as fairly typical. The Long Beach fathers declared as follows:

"No person shall indulge in caresses, hugging, fondling, embracing, spooning, kissing or wrestling with any person or persons of the opposite sex in or upon or near any public park, avenue, street, court, way alley or place, or on the beach, or any other public place . . . and no person shall sit or lie with his or her head, or any other portion of his or her person upon any portion of a person or persons of the opposite sex upon or near any of the said public places."

Provincial. During the season of 1924-25 Los Angeles undertook its first grand opera. The operas were not especially attractive, but the attempt was not to be discouraged, and many were hopeful. Then, on the occasion of the last performance, it seemed necessary that there should be a long moment of self-congratulation. For this purpose the

President, a jurist of local fame, was chosen spokesman, and his pleasant task was that of advertising
all the deacons, elders and dowagers who had made
the supreme sacrifice of opening their homes to con-
spiratory high teas, and had loaned their valuable
names, or their stenographers to the laudable enterprise.

Appropriate pause was made after each illustrious social climber was mentioned, to permit of
enthusiastic hand-clapping from the boxes and the
sycophants of boxes; and after several scores of
souls had thus been made happy, and the eminent
judge was about to make a regretful exit in favor
of an impatient director, a vulgar yokel from the
gallery boomed down the honest query: "Why
don't you drag in the stage hands?" Perhaps the
President of the first opera association would have
done better to have named all the aspiring ladies
of the city whilst he was about it, for it is now announced that a rival organization has been formed
to bestow upon the hungry citizens yet more extensive means of self-display. At present the outlook is very dark.

The same situation exists with regard to the independent theatre. At the close of the late war a few
idealists got together for the purpose of launching
what they called a "Theatre Arts Alliance." A
rather wonderful site was chosen, and thereon, amid
sage-clad hills, was to be built a huge outdoor auditorium for the presentation of Greek drama, concerts and the like. For more intimate purposes, a
part of this greater theatre was to be provided with

means of inclosure, and here not plays alone, but pictures, sculpture and dancing were to have their turn. Around this inspired spot dwellings were to be provided, wherein the artist might dream and create to his soul's content.

It was all very beautiful, very generous; but it required money. Then came the rich lady, with the gift—and the string. The gift was to be substantial, but the string was inevitable. For the lady was also an idealist, and her great dream was of an international, a world religion: and—she had written a play. The theatre was to be a means of religious propaganda, and *her* play was to be the first, and, as it proved, the last consideration.

Because of this the unmystical and pessimistic withdrew in confusion. Later the lady also withdrew and rolled her own. And that is how the Hollywood hills came to have "The Christ Play" for the greater delectation of the fundamentalists,* and their tourist relatives. The original group was left with a large plot of ground and a great outdoor theatre, which is now given over to popular concerts.

Following an example so richly productive of publicity, a number of other ladies organized theatres which have met with more or less ephemeral success. If some plan could be devised whereby every ambitious woman of limited beauty and unlimited wealth could be guaranteed a position of supreme, exalted and undisputed authority for even a single day during the season, no doubt Los An-

* Derived from "fundament."

geles could be assured one of the largest independent theatres in the world.

If the endowed independents have completely failed, the unendowed have fared but little better. After the Ordynski fiasco a few years ago, Mr. Frayne Williams—then just over from a long apprenticeship under St. John Ervine—organized the Literary Theatre, presenting such things as "The Shadow of the Glen," "Hindle Wakes," "John Gabriel Borkman," "The Wild Duck," "The Knight of the Burning Pestle," "The Devil's Disciple" and "Macaire" for more than five seasons. These plays have been skillfully produced under greater than ordinary difficulties, and there have been moderate houses; but the regulars have made it impossible to get adequate hearing, and the populace as a whole has been indifferent. At present, under the auspices of the State University, his enterprise is barely meeting expenses.

Another theatre was beginning to attract attention in 1924, and opened with "The Hairy Ape," and "Six Characters in Search of an Author;" but when the regulars saw that there was danger of its becoming a success, they bought off certain of the leading newspapers, brought pressure to bear upon the owners of the theatre building, and, by depriving them of both advertising and house, firmly put an end to their ambitions. The public moved on in apathetic bewilderment.

But the town is not devoid of amusement, if one knows where to find it. There is the big Methodist pow wow at Trinity Auditorium, with an ath-

letic champion of the Ku Klux Klan before its foot-
lights,— a person with loud voice and enough
absurdity to move the profoundest pessimist to im-
moderate laughter. The Baptist clown does stunts
at the Philharmonic theatre that cause the local
shoe clerks and janitors to jam the doors, and give
the cafeteria hounds hoochless hebie jeebies. The
"Four Square" gospeller—a screeching lady par-
sonette—does a one act that brings joy to thousands. Any one of these three popular fundamentalists is sufficient to insure this city of the sera-
phim against the arrival of Dr. Billy Sunday. We
simply do not need him: our three ring circus is
enough.

Also there are the cults. It is beyond question
that there are more nonsense cults in the environs
of this city than anywhere else on earth.

They were emptied here out of Boston by way
of Chicago. The milder climate enables them to
keep the illusion that they have conquered disease
through spiritual power. They are the sick sur-
vivors of New England transcendentalism, and
while they are no more native than eucalyptus trees,
they provide a sort of comedy that is not without its
merits.

All are here, from the venerable and materially
respectable Christian Scientists on down to the followers of Frater Aleister Crowley, with their il-
luminating rites of black, black magic. Some of
these fakirs have handsome lodges erected at the
expense of gullible millionaires whose intellectual
culture had hitherto been confined to the higher

realms of swine breeding. Many a broken movie queen finds solace in these palaces of opulent optimism.

That the environment is healthy for more honest fakirs is shown by the comparatively recent experience of "General" Nicholas Zogg. This suave gentleman had the insight and courage to select Los Angeles for a rather daring experiment. Here, within a stone's throw of Mexico, he made the claim that he had but recently been one of the leading military commanders in the land of Porfirio Diaz, and, since it had happened that, on the way to some Damascus, the scales had fallen from his eyes, he now desired to become the savior of his most unfortunate country.

He wished to begin reform from the idyllic region of Yucatan, where, he declared, were thousands of Christ-like communists, living in a happy state of brotherly love; where ardent craftsmen, from the sheer love of beauty, created exquisite things from gold and silver and spread them out on the streets for the delight and possession of those who might care to see and take. The country, however, was in sad need of funds.

Dozens of sentimental ladies responded to the gentleman's eloquent prayers, and thousands were raised for the coming civilization. Unfortunately the Federal authorities were in search of the great leader, who was wanted, so it was said, under several names throughout the states. He was literally snatched from the banquet tables of his admiring supporters, who were then ready to follow him into the heart of Central America. General Zogg, it seems, had never spent more than six months in Mexico during his entire life, and was not noticeably proficient in the use of Spanish. It cannot be said that Los Angeles is inhospitable.

Nor is it unliterary. One of the chief methods for measuring the degree of success is the determination of mass production. Just apply it to the business of letters in the precincts of this throbbing California super-town and see what you discover. Living on the fringes of Los Angeles are Upton Sinclair, Edgar Rice Burroughs, Will Levington Comfort, Rupert Hughes and Zane Grey: the combined annual sales of these indefatigible writers will run into millions, and will, I believe, excel the total production of all the novelists east of the Mississippi. Burroughs—author of the Tarzan tales—and Sinclair—author of "The Jungle"—are the most popular of living writers, among the Bolsheviki. And the democratic standards of taste—whatever they are—must ultimately conquer the world: that is, if we are to credit the opinions of the Rotarians. In a recent circular of his, Sinclair announces that Johan Bojer has called him "Master." What reply can a mere American critic make to that?

Mr. H. L. Mencken, not long ago, made the assertion that more manuscripts came into his office from this region than from any other part of the United States: and, recently, a New York literary agent, after taking careful census, came to a similar conclusion. Both authorities make the gesture condemnatory and agree that the bulk of the stuff is rubbish. From this Mr. Mencken infers that Los Angeles is hopeless. That seems to me a very superficial judgment. If it be true that there is such a vast amount of—shall we say it?—scribbling in these parts, it must go to show: 1. That Los Angeles is a degree less materialistic than other American cities of comparable population,—that it contains more idealists. 2. That there is a greater hunger for what is popularly called culture: in a word, more ambition.

That the writing is bad is but an indication that the West is yet unsophisticated. That the stuff exists in such quantities shows that it is not yet blasé and bored. If my conclusions are at all sound it may indicate that this abused region holds much for the future.

In this connection one should, perhaps, point out the fact that for many years Los Angeles, and its immediate environs, has proved itself one of the most appreciative musical centers of North America, and, as a further token of its unmaterialism, its suburban hills are fairly dotted with the palm-thatched studios of budding painters and sculptors.

And now, being somewhat of a bibliophile, I must grow more serious. For not only has the Huntington library come to the city gates; not only do the city walls hem in the largest collections of Dryden and Oscar Wilde in the world: but Los Angeles alone has the distinction of harboring the most excellent book shops in all the West.

To begin at the bottom, two of the largest de-

partment stores—Robinson's and Bullock's—have
sections that will compare favorably, both as to the
extent and quality of stock, with Marshall Field's
in Chicago and Brentano's in New York. Parker's
is one of the best places to buy new books in America, and he one of the most intelligent of the old
style bookmen.

Besides a half dozen other shops for new books
there are nearly a score of second hand stalls that
boast of more old books than any similar places
west of New York. Dawson's is a place for rare
books, where a certain air of old-worldiness persists
in spite of the realtors and progressives. Except
on the Atlantic coast he has no worthy competitor
in the States. Moreover, one doesn't need to pine
for Rosenbach's or George D. Smith's when one
can conveniently drop into George M. Millard's
exquisite collection of first editions, Kelmscotts and
incunabula in the suburb of Pasadena. If one may
judge by symptoms there is more reading and more
discrimination in reading in Los Angeles than in
San Francisco. Parker claims, I believe, never to
have handled a novel by Harold Bell Wright.

Well, there you have it. A rare mixture—of
evangelical mountebanks, new thoughters, swamis,
popular novelists, movie persons, solemn pamphlet-
eers, realtors, ku kluxers, joiners of the thou-
sand-and-one fraternal orders of good will and
everlasting sunshine, artists, consumptives, music
lovers, cripples, retired farmers, ex beer magnates,
—mostly American to the core, and as typical as
sign boards and peanut stands. There is the old

Plaza, the most interesting bit remaining, swarming with impoverished Mexicans and thrifty Japanese; towering hills in the mid-city, still bearing the decaying houses of the old pioneers: the shifting business district, looking, for all the world, like St. Louis or Milwaukee: and the outlying heights, stretching toward Hollywood or the sea, and covered now with new palaces in Italian villa, French Renaissance, or Hopi Indian architecture for the pleasuring of the plutocrats. In the midst of this strange hish-hash is the largest woman's club in America, and the greatest number of God-fearing Puritans.

A few rebels look on and sneer, but their sneers are unobserved. The crowd surges by, seizing frantically at the uplift pamphlets handed out by fagged and sad-eyed women for the enhancement of the town-boomers: "Take a free ride to Eve's Garden, the Gigantic new subdivision planned for you by Fawn and Leach, the Realty Kings. Absolutely Free!"

And yet, the bug of optimism seizes me; I succumb. It is now my firm conviction, Mencken notwithstanding, that out of this motley throng of goose-steppers and propagandists there will grow the most splendid center of genuine culture and enlightenment on this continent. For, with all its uncouthness, the place is alive with illusions, and illusions are the stuff of art.

CHEYENNE:

THE WILD WEST SELLS ITS ATMOSPHERE
By
Cary Abbott

CHEYENNE

SHORTLY after the Birth of a Nation had been achieved, another smaller but violent parturition took place in what was then Dakota Territory in 1867. Of all the hectic origins of the Western cities, Cheyenne's was the most thrilling. Even those communities which have a similar beginning concede to Cheyenne its premier position as the worst of the tough towns. Many conservative people who have endured life there since the early days have tried to live down this wild start, but they can do little about it but deplore the fact that most of America still believes that Cheyenne is a thoroughly "bad" place.

It may be as respectable, attractive, and synthetically sophisticated a place as ever spawned a country club. Nevertheless, romantic legend persists in painting the town "red." Cheyenne must be wide-open, cowboys shooting up the main street, vigilantes hanging desperadoes by the dozen, Jezebels playing Lorelei from the front porch, Indians and cattle kicking up dust in the outskirts, etc, etc.

Unfortunately for those who crave "atmosphere," Cheyenne is, and has been for years, devoid of these attractions. Drinking is only carried on in bathrooms and alleys as is customary all over the United States; cowboys, except during the Frontier show, come to town in automobiles wearing the quietest possible clothes; the nearest Indians doze through life a couple of hundred miles away, unless exhibiting their paint and feathers in Hollywood or London for a consideration; the cattle no longer rove the illimitable spaces, but are tended, nursed and dipped for various ailments like pet dogs or canaries; denizens (good old euphemism of the journals!) of the tenderloin are no longer denizens, as such; vigilantes' committees were long ago replaced by the ponderous though less efficacious law; nothing of the old West is left but the dust, and even that is being conquered by paved roads and grain crops. Even the wind, the unforgettable Rocky Mountain Zephyr hymned by Bill Nye and cursed by everyone else,—even the wind has lost its virility.

Yet the legend of the ideal tough Western town lives on. Surely, Cheyenne must have been a fearful affair in 1867, when the Union Pacific Railroad stopped its westward building operations there for the winter. When the railroad land agent staked out his quarters against the simultaneous arrival of the construction gang and the winter, all of the flotsam and a good deal of the jetsam of humanity who had been following up the Union Pacific as it was moving west, moved from Julesburg, Colorado, their last place of revelry. This aggregation moved up to Cheyenne on flat-cars, and the spectacle of all these wild

characters and camp-followers of divers shady
professions traveling in this al fresco manner
earned the beautiful and appropriate name of
"Hell on Wheels."

With this crew of holy terrors there arrived of
course all sorts and conditions of people,—railroad
men, soldiers, bull-whackers who were hauling the
ways and means to set up winter quarters for the
crowd, plainsmen, cowmen, settlers adventuring
for the first time into the great West. Shacks,
tents, dug-outs and a few more or less permanent
structures arose out of the treeless prairie to form
the semblance of a town. As the winter progressed, the motley and volatile population
amused itself in the manner beloved by all readers
of fiction and all the "hounds" for Western
movies. The vices all flourished, scarlet and unrestrained. Shootings and murders occurred with
delightful frequency.

Expensive, too, all this joy was, even by post-
war standards. At McDaniel's theater, which was
really a dance hall, admission was gained by tossing a dollar into the barrel at the door, which
each morning was rolled off to a bank to be
emptied.

It was a place, likewise, for the grandiose and
romantic in gesture. Especially of virile friendship. An Old Timer spent two thirds of a long
life entertaining a tamer Cheyenne with an oc-
currence which made McDaniel's even more
famous than its general reputation for genial
bawdiness. The Old Timer, then young, stood

in the place one night beside a post in a far corner of the main hall. Gambling raged. Thirsty males roared and whined their orders over a full bar. A score of fresh-painted damsels shrieked and postured suggestivities from the stage. It was a large night, in short, and nobody thinking about cemeteries.

Then suddenly two shots boomed. They came in that curiously swift sequence which, to the sophisticated, advertised that a two-gun man was plying his art. My Old Timer thought swiftly and painfully of cemeteries, as his left ear tingled from a bullet's wind, and then his right.

The Old Timer always concluded the account—and probably still does wherever in Elysium bedtime stories are told to the children of the Homeric heroes—this way:

"When that fust shot come, I was skeert somebody was trying to pick me off. But when that second bullit just grazed my right ear, I knew it was just my ole friend Bill playin' a joke on me."

And sure enough it was, for the tale is fairly well authenticated. Bill had come up from the wilder rural regions, and caught sight of my Old Timer before the Old Timer had seen Bill. So he played this gorgeous parody of the children's game of coming up from behind, clapping hands over the eyes of an unsuspecting one and making him "guess who this is." Bill made the Old Timer "guess who this was" by the way he shot. Such were the frolics of friendship in Cheyenne in the

careless '60's. Foes were more careful only in
that they took pains to shoot within the circle
bounded by the ears.

However, after the worst element became too
free with other people's lives and money, in absence of law machinery, a vigilantes' committee
began the genial task of ridding the community
of a number of the more callous gunmen. My
sister's godmother, arriving as a bride at night,
saw, as her first glimpse of the golden West by
daylight, two men hanging by their necks to a
telegraph pole,—the successful result of the vigilantes' handiwork. Even after the territory was
organized, a mob one night clamored for the life
of some particularly wicked character, and in spite
of the pleas of the newly-made mayor and the
thunders of the United States attorney, the crowd
had to have its blood, and the desperado was duly
lynched.

In the spring the railroad went on its way westward, leaving the town to its fate. Unlike many
Western towns with such hectic beginnings,
Cheyenne's geographic position made it permanent. Shortly the Union Pacific built a line
to Denver from there, as Cheyenne was the nearest point to the metropolis of the mining craze.
Freighting outfits found Cheyenne a convenient
center to haul to the Black Hills, to South Pass
City where gold was exciting interest, even into
Montana. Between Cheyenne and the neighboring army post a great depot called Camp Carlin
made its appearance, furnishing supplies to all the

numerous garrisons which at one time dotted the
West.

To be sure, after the first winter, when about
six thousand people milled about like cattle on the
bleak town site, the population dwindled as the
greater part of the rag-tag and bobtail moved on
with the railroad. Nevertheless, enough stayed to
realize that money was to be made in the new distributing center for the future Territory, and that
cattle could be raised profitably in this grassy
wilderness. With the continual pouring of settlers into the West after the Civil War, Cheyenne
perpetually overflowed with adventurous souls, as
fitted a self-confessed gateway to the unknown
and boundless West.

Lots sold for outrageous prices, stores, banks,
schools and churches sprang up. Dwelling-houses
and a gorgeous and more sybaritic type of saloon
appeared. A court-house was erected, a building
now destroyed to make way for a "bigger and better" one; but the old court-house had a history as
interesting as its appearance was hideous. So
quickly did the town erect itself that it earned the
name of "the Magic City." The place was incorporated. The territory was carved out of the
mammoth Dakota and other vague empires, and
organized. A capitol building then became necessary but pending the territory's ability to erect
it, the first legislatures held their sessions in the
second story of a frame house. A handful of
boosting and outwardly conventional persons arrived—precursors of the Babbitts of the 1920's.

Meanwhile, hardy pioneers and plainsmen had established, or were establishing themselves in various strategic places over the country, starting the cattle industry in a modest way, which in a few years was to become the paramount industry of the plains, wild and Indian-infested as they were. Cheyenne was almost the center of this region where great herds were trailed up from Texas or driven out from the country to the east—a region abominated by the great cow barons because cattle in large quantities could not thrive there, owing to the cutting up of lands for farms. Out in Wyoming Territory, the cattle ranged at large, identified only by the owners' brands, and rounded up once or twice a year. The wide, open-air life of the range, combined with the rising price of cattle on eastern markets, began to draw young and aristocratic bloods from our Eastern seaboard and even from England and Scotland. As a large majority of the cattle destined for market were driven into the Cheyenne stockyards for shipment, Cheyenne became the headquarters for the industry.

Freedom from the conventions of more civilized communities throve in this high and windy atmosphere. There were no uplift movements, no elaborate programs of brotherly love to hamper one's inclinations in those days. The cattlemen, both the pioneer, plainsman type, who had exchanged pot-shots with Indians and outlaws and the scions of refinement and old-world wealth, met on common and frequently hilarious ground. The

Cheyenne Club became a social center such as has never since been approached in the West, and rarely elsewhere. During the eighties, when the cattle business was at its height, and the profits from the great companies, whose herds ranged from Canada to Texas, were tremendous, the cattle kings had little to do but spend their money wildly and enjoy liberty.

Fine horseflesh was the fashion. The streets of the capital city of Wyoming were alive with turnouts of all descriptions. Horses from Kentucky, thoroughbreds and Irish hunters, cayuses and wild-eyed plugs cavorted bravely through the streets. Tallyhoes, phaetons, traps, landaus, broughams mingled with vulgar chuck wagons, stage-coaches and the various noisy and springless contraptions that still find favor in the army. A race-course was built. Members of the Club jockeyed their own races and afterward repaired to the clubhouse where something was enjoyed resembling 19th hole festivities raised to the nth power. The prize, which was always a large silver cup made at Tiffany's, then became the nucleus for a champagne party. The Club's parties were as famous as the membership, and to-day one may see the bullet-hole in a painting of a bull by Paul Potter, the proud scar of an exciting night.

A lady, noted alike for her horses and her wig, became embroiled one day in a bet with a bank president as to who owned the faster animal. After much argument, they decided to race to the

middle of town, about half a mile distant. As
the horses tore through the business streets to the
goal, the lady's hat and wig flew off, but she won
the race and the bet. It was said that the wig
had flown off to allow her the victor's bay leaves.
There were classicists in early Cheyenne who understood such matters. But the populace scowled
sardonically at the pretentious jest and parodied
it with the quip that the lady had won the bay
rum bottle.

Fort Russell people, usually keen on horses,
had one officer in those days, who showed strange
knowledge of how to hitch up a horse. Very at-
tentive to a town lady, one night he invited her
to the post to a hop. Arriving at her house after
dark, he escorted her to the waiting carriage. On
the way, she noticed that the horse seemed to be
moving in a curious manner, and thought perhaps
that it had partaken of a trifle too much as had her
partner. However, on coming into the glare of
light in front of the Post Hall, the poor horse
was discovered by the much delighted throng to
be hitched to the carriage in such a way that the
animal was astraddle one shaft!

Conviviality was rampant, and the gossip of the
times was built on many merry episodes. Matrimony arrived even during the railroad epoch, but
did not always go hand in hand with the plateau's
new freedoms. There is a tale of a prominent cattleman who, arriving at his house after a protracted "tear," was greeted by a bellicose wife
armed with two pistols. It was several weeks be-

fore he was allowed to enter his domain. Even
this affair did not cure him. Before long, he was
in his cups again. Next morning his wife was seen
throwing all his clothes and belongings into the
front yard. When asked the why and wherefore,
she replied that he had been at it again, and that
he was going to sleep in the barn indefinitely. This
impatient Griselda has a window to her memory
in one of Cheyenne's churches.

Whatever happened to the two men who were
trundled home in a wheelbarrow by a third partner in crime, no one has ever heard. The three
had been "whooping it up" at the Club until number three was the only survivor. He deemed it
proper to see that his friends got home to their
respective and probably irate wives, so he used this
means of getting them there. But after he had
thrown number one out at his door and rung the
bell, he was nearly exhausted. So when he came
to number two's house, he simply left him to
bivouac, as it were, on his own stoop.

There is the story of a young and festive cattleman, who rode over two hundred miles by relay
into Cheyenne to see Lily Langtry play at the
opera house Having accomplished this much, he
became a sort of Lochinvar, and went on with
the Jersey Lily to the Coast.

The first sight to greet the eyes of a newcomer
one day was a tallyho in full cry at the station.
The passengers seemed to be busy trying to stay
on the vehicle with bad success. It was whispered
that these irrational persons were a crowd of

England's bluest. At any rate, at this time, a daughter of one of the heads of a great cattle company (girls were scarce in those days, and had a most wonderful time), on being patronized by some superior person, informed her that she need not give herself such airs, as the night before she herself had sat down to dinner in her father's house, the only girl with six British peers.

Numerous social crises betray the somewhat pioneer state of things in the palmy days. The wife of the governor, who was away somewhere, heard that the President of the United States was to stop in Cheyenne. Her train and the President's were to come in at the same time, giving her no time to prepare herself for the honor of entertaining him. There was nothing she could do about it except to change her clothes in the baggage car, her train being one of the old-fashioned variety that often carried no Pullmans. She did, and the President heard all about it at the reception.

One old settler who had to make the stage trip to Deadwood often became frightened at the prospect of being shot by a road-agent who had been recently raiding all Black Hills-bound traffic. But he had to go, so he made his wife go with him, and she carried nearly twenty thousand dollars in gold on her person destined for a Deadwood bank, all because her timorous husband hoped the bandit might let the women go unmolested. There is no climax to this tale, as the lady was the only sufferer, since she had the gloomy pleasure of having all that weight fastened on her fore and aft. She may well have been the deified ancestress of the modern wife who, also to protect her husband and his Cadillac, rides through cordons of woman-hood-revering prohibition agents with Scotch bottles dangling more or less imperceptibly from her girdle. But the old breed was sturdier. Quite obviously it had greater heft.

Money flowed fast in the eighties. A proof is in the short career of two brothers who had been sent out from England by an irate father with one million dollars on condition they would not darken the ancestral doors again. At the end of their first year, which was spent on a great ranch, and enlivened with wine, women, and all the ex-travagances possible to wealth in the eighties, they had "shot their wad" and, returning to England, were given another million, which they took to South Africa. Evidently these Alexanders had found another world to conquer, or the campaign turned out to be less brief; at any rate, they never returned to Wyoming.

But what can one expect of a town whose gilded youth danced cotillions at ten o'clock in the morning? Perhaps the fact that Cheyenne was the first town in the world to have electric lights had something to do with it. Our age of electricity is characterized by mad restlessness; and possibly the presence of this element had its effect on the gay inhabitants of the little Western city who dined and gambled and got drunk under the "bright lights," before gas-mains were laid. Cer-

THE LAST TRIP OF THE CHEYENNE-DEADWOOD COACH ON FEBRUARY 19, 1887

tain it is that the little electric plant used to have
a hard time puffing up enough current to keep
the lights going for those who insisted on turning
night into day.

As for luxuries, Cheyenne had fine stores, and
a far better discrimination for this world's delights
than nowadays. Several times, when someone
wished to have such delicacies as fresh fish or oysters at a dinner-party, or whatever might be in
season back in the States, he had these things
sent out by express in freight-cars packed in ice,
a formidable undertaking before these days of
refrigerator systems on railroads. One dinner for
twenty people, given as a sort of thank-offering re-
garding the successful outcome of a transaction in
cattle, cost five thousand dollars. And those were
the days when dollar-a-plate dinners were considered an extravagance as far west as Kansas
City!

There is another side to the picture of Cheyenne
in the cattle days, of course. While there were
those who furnished more than enough "pepper,"
there have always been conservative, quiet "salt
of the earth" type of people, who have kept the
balance of business and community life, some deploring the spectacular life of the gilded ones,
others making their stakes without ostentation and
smiling at the gay crowd, even as ants grinned
at the sluggard. While the fine arts could hardly
have been said to have flourished, a number of
splendid homes were built, the new Capitol arose,
and the usual schools and churches.

Sometimes a regenerated magnifico lurched spectacularly from one side to the other.

A prominent cattle king who had "got religion" sufficiently to be desirous of baptism, invited a large party to witness his immersion in the tank at the Baptist Church. Unfortunately, either the Lord was not with him or the waterworks were not functioning. The tank obstinately refused to fill. So the baptism was postponed till another day; and, anticlimactical as it might be, all the friends gathered again, as they were determined not to miss the fun on any account.

Another important gentleman, whose religious feelings had not been suspected by his closest friends, gave a stained window to a new church. When he was asked by some highly surprised crony as to how he, of all people, happened to do such a thing, he replied: "Why, I'm one of the pillars of the damn thing!"

Thus passed Cheyenne's glory. During the fearful winters at the end of the eighties, many fortunes made in cattle or in promoters' paper collapsed. As cattle were unfenced, and allowed to shift largely for themselves, except for occasional roundups, the succession of severe snowstorms drove them to their death by starvation or suffocation in the drifts. Thousands and thousands of head perished, while human help was useless and futile. The "great open spaces" have a horribly seamy side, and eight months of winter is the seamiest, as any cattleman knows. The cattle bubble was pricked, and those who had family or means to fly to for aid did so, while others braved poverty. The business of cattle raising continues to this day, but on a smaller and far more careful scale. Only a very few outfits nowadays can begin to be compared to the baronial holdings common thirty and more years ago.

One of the last, and certainly the most picturesque performance which the cattlemen undertook in concert was the campaign conducted to root out from the land the small settlers and homesteaders. These people, who had been filtering into the country in the natural course of events, were looked at with wrath, as they were taking up lands in fertile districts, and cutting up the unfenced domain, thus hindering the free movements of the great herds. They were also suspected of "rustling," and with plenty of reason. Therefore, the plot was woven secretly, and suddenly a large number of the cattle kings, with their various gunmen and riders left for the north.

Johnson County, three hundred miles away, was the goal for this organized attack on the small potatoes; and the country was to be freed by force, if necessary, of new settlers and the desperadoes who stole the mavericks of the big companies. Because of the prominence of many of the plotters, the true story of this now ancient tale of truculence has never been properly told. The accounts vary a good deal as to the victims of the affair, some of whom were killed and others spirited out of the region. The dramatic surrounding of the cattlemen by the "rustlers" and their timely rescue by troops caused unheard-of excitement. This was followed by the technical arrest of the crowd of "invaders" by Government troops, and the raid ended farcically.

Popular feeling, at first against the cattle interests, veered suddenly. The raiders were brought back to Cheyenne, and held in a very courteous imprisonment in a corral at Fort Russell. Soon even this mild detention, through mysterious means in Washington, ended. Furthermore, not a court would have convicted them, so strong had become the sympathy of the people in their favor. During their "incarceration," the prisoners found it quite easy to get furloughs to go in to Cheyenne for business and pleasure. The Government in those days could not take too seriously the assumed rights of a breezy and wealthy crowd of men in a remote country, up till this time practically policed and controlled by such pioneers. The Johnson County "invasion," however, was regarded seriously enough to warrant the secret buying up of a book telling much too much, and thereby hurting some financial and political careers. As is usual with such publications, a few copies saw the light, and are to this day guarded with traditional secrecy.

Politics had much to do with the *dénouement* of the raid, but then politics have been meat and drink, particularly drink, to Cheyenne, as being a capital from the beginning of things in Wyoming. Many people who point to Cheyenne's noble citizenry as the great-hearted souls who first gave women full suffrage, do not know what a mighty wrangling took place on the subject in the shaky old two-storied building where the first Solons, bearded far more than the pard, thrashed out this weighty subject. It has been said that the real reason why women were allowed to vote at that time was because of the paucity of inhabitants of the territory, and the consequent desire to swell the number of votes cast for ambitious candidates. This is related to the manner in which Cheyenne's census was taken in later years,—by going through the transcontinental trains at the station and taking down the necessary data from passengers, which unwittingly made them citizens of a town they had inhabited for about twenty minutes.

Later years proved that women in Cheyenne were not so proud of voting. For many elections, the politicians could only get them to vote by sending the old-fashioned "hired" hacks around to their homes to take them to the polls. This method finally became anathema to the sore-heads of a continuously defeated party, and was made unlawful. By that time, too, the old hacks were so redolent of livery stables and departed drunks that many women declined the honor of a free ride, anyway.

One of the most delightful scenes that the newly completed Capitol building witnessed was the spectacle of a new governor, who, finding his normal entrance to his office barricaded by a predecessor disputing the election, made his *joyeuse entrée* by means of a ladder through a window!

Cheyenne has always been unpopular politically through the state, because, being for years the center of government, she has doled out the various state institutions to the rising young commonwealths. Here the insane asylum, there the home for adenoid sufferers, yon the reformatory or the experimental station where lambs lie down with lions in the most up-to-date manner. The original five immense counties have been butchered into many smaller ones to make county seats for office-seekers to find offices. As railroads gradually built their cautious way across the wide areas of Wyoming, Cheyenne, although in a far corner, became the only logical place to foregather for meetings of residents from the scattered settlements and towns. Cheyenne, for some obscure reason, has never been the fixed capital; and every few years an agitation starts to move the seat of government to some other place. The last time that Cheyenne was contemplating what it would do with its big Capitol building, a handful of the tried "old hands" quietly put through a measure in the legislature to appropriate a huge sum to enlarge the building for added office room. Thus, before the agitators were aware of their work, the state was saddled with a bigger and better Capitol,—now too costly an affair to move for years to come.

During the nineties, Cheyenne lost her glamour as the uncrowned capital of the wild and woolly

West. Railroads had put an end to the vast freighting business. With the decline of the Indian into innocuous desuetude, the numerous little army posts were, one after another, dismantled, and Camp Carlin was left to decay. The hard winters, together with a slump in cattle prices, had wrought ruin to the great cattle companies, and the smaller ranchers gradually took over their lands. Sheep, too, made their appearance, much to the wrath of cattle-growers. Irrigation of lands for farming was initiated. The handwriting was on the wall for those to whom Cheyenne under the old order of life had been the rule.

To-day, the "spirit of the West" is a somewhat sickly old man, carefully tended and nursed along to keep alive the old spark. Cheyenne is horribly afraid that some day the "spirit" will die. Hence the now nationally famous and much advertised institution known as the Frontier Days celebration. The idea of this, the oldest of all the now numerous "Wild West" shows, the "daddy of them all," as reads the slogan (the old West submits to a slogan like everybody else these days), sprang from a highly informal and immensely entertaining afternoon in 1897.

A group of citizens whose like is to be found in all communities, decided to get together a number of the old cowhands and ranchers to put on an exhibition, or rather contest, to show their skill in roping steers, riding wild horses and trying their luck in a few races on cow-ponies. To give the affair a little atmosphere, one of the old stage-coaches used in the Deadwood days was hauled out of its half-forgotten resting-place, some Shoshone and Arapahoe Indians were brought down from their reservation on flat-cars, and some cavalry from Fort Russell was borrowed. The prizes for the contests were simple, and the show did not pretend to be more than an afternoon's amusement. As the grandstand was small, people went out very early, to insure getting seats, taking their lunches along. The show was sufficiently good to warrant another one the following year. Before the town was aware of the fact, the splendid work of those marvelous horsemen of the plains in these early celebrations became known to neighboring states, and the show was staged annually.

These early performances had many of the faults of amateurish management. Long delays between races and contests, combined with sudden dramatic climaxes unlooked for by the management, made the afternoons in the grandstand or on horseback in the arena both boring and thrilling. Occasionally a steer would climb over all possible obstacles apparently burning to gore everyone in sight. Sometimes a broncho would insist on kicking his way into the middle of next week. The Indian squaw races were always delightful, as the Shoshone women were immense, while their mounts were thin little things, with a habit of turning corners suddenly and upsetting their huge riders. The climax of the earlier shows was the pursuit of the stage-coach around the track by Indians, to be finally rescued by the cavalry and cowboys.

One year saw the coach loaded with the Secretary of Agriculture and other notables together with some ladies. The stage horses, frightened by the yells of the Indians and the revolvers and six shooters popping, got beyond the control of the driver and tore around the track in magnificent style. The stage careened beautifully, all the ladies shrieked, the Indians whooped, and the cavalry had a hard run to make good the proper end of the act. Everyone who saw it was immensely pleased, and only sorry that a massacre had not been committed to round the performance off in good order.

As the years passed, riders from more and more distant places came to compete for the honors at Cheyenne. The show became an affair of more than one day, due to the necessity of giving contestants a fair chance to "do their stuff." As more and more people came to see the Frontier Days, the gate receipts made it possible to offer large prizes of money. Saddles have from the beginning been donated by the Union Pacific Railroad to the winners of the bucking contest, and other trophies have been offered at various shows. Gradually the older men who rode and raced and hogtied steers to make the holiday a success gave place to the younger generation who had been born and brought up in the saddle. Other towns emulated Cheyenne's show, and soon these boys began moving from one show to the next. To-day riding at these numerous celebrations is almost a profession, many of the performers not being native to the West and knowing little about the business of ranching as it used to be practiced.

The show to-day is a great and glorious athletic contest, full of thrills and life, all sorts of *divertissements* being used to attract attention which had no part nor place in the ranch life of the cattle ranges. Fancy roping, acrobatics on horseback such as the Cossacks of Buffalo Bill's show used to do, complicated drills by cavalry, etc., etc. The now indispensable "bull-dogging" of steers is another importation, a stunt which a negro from Texas brought into the program one year. This man used to fasten his teeth in the nostrils of the steer, and by the power of his neck and jaws turn the animal over on its side. Nobody pretends to do that any more; it is thrilling enough to see a man jump from his horse to the steer's neck and twist him over by his horns.

The crowd which patronizes the show to-day is of course the automobile tourist horde. They see four or five days of perfectly managed, amazingly wonderful horsemanship of all sorts. The grounds are well-kept, steel grandstand, parking for automobiles, all the necessities of taking care of a multitude.

But as the stranger sits in the upper stand looking out over the arena and paddock, filled with the tumultuous movement of horses, Indians, soldiers, cowboys, all in the full panoply of their various professions, and then gazes beyond to the city buried in summer greenery, with its golden dome and church towers and array of houses and buildings reaching the long red line of the Fort Russell barracks and quarters, does it occur to him that in the whole area there is only one livery stable,—one inn for the stranger's plug to be put up for the night? Does the guest of the city realize that if he stayed a month after the show he would hardly see a man on horseback in the streets of the "capital of the cow country?" Does he know that those Indians who are leaping about in front of the grandstand in a war-dance use aniline dyes to make themselves so gorgeous? That the Indians, the steers, the horses, the riders are hired under contract? In other words, that this spectacle can hardly be said to be the spontaneous, untamed, gladhand West of the days that Owen Wister and Buffalo Bill and General Custer and Bill Nye and Colonel Roosevelt made immortal?

Out of the acorn of 1897 a great oak has matured; and because of the demand for "Western" atmosphere, the Cheyenne show will last for many years. The business of being wild and woolly is highly lucrative these days. The riders make good money, the Indians have excellent pay and a wonderful time showing off, the contractors for the livestock get their rake-off, the city, which owns the show, managed through the Chamber of Commerce, gets both money and quantities of publicity. One will see many people on the streets at Frontier time wearing boots and spurs and, above all, the "ten-gallon" hats (a style imported into Wyoming in recent years, and in no manner resembling the less flamboyant and more practical hats of twenty years ago), who, if they had to mount a horse immediately, would try to get on the wrong side or else discreetly flee.

All this fol-de-rol is part of the "Western" spirit, resurrected in a form palatable to the great American public, whose appetite for Western "life" has been fed continually since the days of "The Virginian" by fiction and the movies.

To the old-timer, viewing the same scene, the old picture of Cheyenne reverts to his mind occasionally, and, being human he thanks God that life is easier these days, creature comforts as much a part of Cheyenne as of any other city with a modern Chamber of Commerce, a country club and paved streets. A generation ago, there were few trees and they were all seedy-looking little things, much abused by the everlasting wind of cursed memory; the Capitol dome, just finished, looked rather lonely at the edge of a wind-swept, sun-bathed town, huddled around the railroad yards; Fort Russell was a compact but tiny circle of buildings off to the west. Yet there are times when "old-timer" will sigh for the days when to have a sense of humor was far more necessary than to have a bath; when horses spent the days and often the nights tied up at the hitching posts and rings down town, their owners busy drawing three of a kind or yelling "keno!" or taking on a few fingers of "licker." The Dyer House and

the Inter-Ocean no longer shine brightly for the
fellow who has just spent a weary three days in
a stage or on horseback; the Opera house has disappeared where Modjeska and Patti and Ada
Rehan once enraptured audiences that wore silk
hats as well as six-shooters; Sir Horace Plunkett
in far-off Ireland is no longer on the board of
governors of the Club; even the days when Roosevelt, on his vice-presidential campaign, left his
train and rode 60 miles by horseback to Cheyenne
to make a speech, are dim to most.

Changes in the West came violently. All the
above rigmarole is myth and legend to many inhabitants. Many people are indifferent to the traditions and history of the communities where they
come to dwell. Those who drift with the vast
tide of humanity who make of the United States
a land of nomads, hardly stay in a place long
enough to absorb the whys and wherefores of the
community. Many Western cities have acquired
in their short lives much history and background,
which is to be had for the asking from the now
fast disappearing pioneers and earlier settlers.
Cheyenne, especially, has been fortunate in the
number of interesting people who have survived
the exciting decades of the cattle period.

Yet what a contrast to their yarns is the life
of to-day. Your modern cowhand comes to town
in a Pullman and gets a room and bath at the
Plains Hotel. Road-shows do their turn in a
movie-house,—Modjeska wouldn't draw a cor-
poral's guard in Cheyenne or any other American

town nowadays!—The Cheyenne Club is now, alas! the abode of the Chamber of Commerce, where Frontier Day performances are cooked up, and where there is a "rest-room" for women automobile tourists; Rooseveltian-mannered Presidents do not await their hostess in the hall, amusing themselves by putting on war-bonnets that happen to adorn the room,—Presidents to-day are apt to be fêted with a special Frontier show just as are trainloads of Shriners or luncheon clubs or groups of magnates who have made the front page in the newspapers.

So Cheyenne passes to-day, the exponent supreme of the wild and woolly West. Dairy herds, dry farms, prohibition officers, the Y. W. C. A.,—progress, uplift, brotherly love—all rampant. It is just one more attractive, highly standardized American city. Except for the ever ingenious youth of the community, who can occasionally work up considerable atmosphere redolent of the old days and ways, only two incidents have happened in recent years which recall the old West.

One night, while a blizzard raged madly, a man struggling through the snow was suddenly confronted with two buffaloes. These belonged to a showman of the city, had got away from their moorings, so to speak, and were wandering helplessly about. He who met these ghosts of yesterday was, of course, accused of "having 'em again."

The other incident was the entertaining of the

"lady" who was traveling with the scion of a famous French banking family, by means of a luncheon at the Country Club. Only in Cheyenne could that happen.